men and the art of
QUILTMAKING

JOE CUNNINGHAM

American Quilter's Society
P. O. Box 3290 • Paducah, KY 42002-3290
www.AmericanQuilter.com

Located in Paducah, Kentucky, the American Quilter's Society (AQS) is dedicated to promoting the accomplishments of today's quilters. Through its publications and events, AQS strives to honor today's quiltmakers and their work and to inspire future creativity and innovation in quiltmaking.

EXECUTIVE BOOK EDITOR: ANDI MILAM REYNOLDS
GRAPHIC DESIGN: ELAINE WILSON
COVER DESIGN: MICHAEL BUCKINGHAM
PHOTOGRAPHY: CHARLES R. LYNCH, UNLESS OTHERWISE NOTED

Additional copies of this book may be ordered from the American Quilter's Society, PO Box 3290, Paducah, KY 42002-3290, or online at www.AmericanQuilter.com.

Text © 2010, Author, Joe Cunningham
Artwork © 2010, American Quilter's Society

Library of Congress Cataloging-in-Publication Data
Cunningham, Joe.
  Men and the art of quiltmaking / by Joe Cunningham.
    p. cm.
  Includes index.
  ISBN 978-1-57432-676-5
  1. Quilting--Patterns--History. 2. Quilts--United States--History. 3.
Quiltmakers--United States. I. Title.
  TT835.C856 2010
  746.46--dc22
                    2010030545

COVER: SNAKE IN THE GARDEN, detail. Full quilt on pages 18 and 83.
TITLE PAGE: UP THE STREAM OF GOOD INTENTIONS, detail. Full quilt on page 71.
RIGHT: WAKAN KCI YU ZAPI SINA, detail. Full quilt on page 22.

DEDICATION

This book is
dedicated to the
memory of
Joseph Hedley
of Warden, England,
1750–1830,
known to his friends
as
Joe the Quilter.

44

46

CONTENTS

48

51

52

54

56

58

60

62

66

FALLING BLOCKS, 74½" x 90½", 1964. Made by
Ernest B. Haight (1899-1986), David City, Nebraska.

men and the art of QUILTMAKING ▸◂ JOE CUNNINGHAM

INTRODUCTION

Before the colonial era in the western hemisphere, men were involved in quilts all the way through, from weaving and dyeing to printing and designing the fabric. English businessmen drove the market by ordering palampores by the thousands from India in the 17th century. Tailors in Europe made quilted cotton bedcovers for the market to satisfy demand in England and France.

But when quilting took hold in the American colonies, it became a strictly female pursuit. There were always the odd few men who took it up, and no doubt more husbands helped their wives than we will ever know, but the DNA of American quilts was encoded as "female." In the same way, American quilts came to be defined as gifts, a quality that also tended to ward off male involvement.

As a man who came of age during the '60s and '70s, however, I did not feel particularly transgressive or mutinous as a male quilter. With all the talk of equality, all the focus on the ways that women could enter realms that were previously closed to them, it did not seem that weird that I might find myself in a territory previously occupied solely by women. I just assumed I was in the vanguard of what would eventually become a vast movement.

Oh, how wrong I was. Today—more than 30 years after I set up shop as a quilter—men still occupy only a tiny corner of "Quiltland" as quilters, although they continue to be the majority heads of the medium-to-large scale business end of things. But two factors have combined to make men more visible, and perhaps to bring more men into the field.

The first is the longarm quilting machine. Quilting machines are, well, machines, and machines tend to attract men. Second is the Internet, which makes it easier for men to find other male quilters, to see that each man is not alone, and to explore quilting in the comfort of a solo journey. Now when I travel around the country for lectures and workshops I nearly always run into men I have met over the Internet.

One of my early heroes was Ernest B. Haight of David City, Nebraska (1899-1986), who made quilts for fifty years, from 1936 to 1986. My friend Julie Silber owns one of his quilts and has been kind enough to lend it for this book (page 6). As you can see, Ernest was not shy about signing his quilts.

I made my first quilt in 1979, then spent more than a decade copying old quilts and learning from older quilters. You can see from the quilt on the cover, SNAKE IN THE GARDEN, which I made in 2000, how deeply influenced I have been by traditional quilt colors and formats. Since about 2005, however, I have found that I want to make quilts that are not nearly so overtly aligned with tradition, and have found my own ways of designing and making quilts.

I had always resisted the idea of becoming known as a "male quilter." It seemed somehow demeaning to think I would have anything in common with another quilter just because we were both the same gender. Once I started calling guys to interview them for this book, however, I began to feel like we were brothers of the quilt. Plenty of times it seemed like I knew what a man was going to say before he said it.

In writing *Men and the Art of Quiltmaking*, it has been a joy to visit with some of my old friends in the business, to make new ones, and to learn how many more men are out there quilting. Of course, this book is only a sampling of men and the art of quiltmaking. My fondest wish is that it lead to a second volume.

Joe Cunningham 2010

Bob Adams

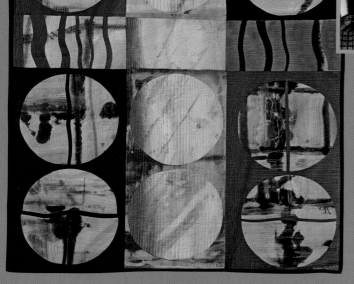

LUNAR No. 2, 32" x 36", 2005

PHOTO: NATALIE ADAMS

Bob's First Quilt

My son needed a bedspread anyway, so I took on a Nine-Patch. At that time my biggest problem was that I didn't know how to operate a sewing machine. My wife would tell me just enough to get going, then something would go wrong and I would have to quit. After I finished the Nine-Patch, I said, how in the world does anybody enjoy doing this? It's like a production line, sewing this square to that square.

The Importance of Teachers

I took a class from Roberta Horton in Denver. She was a good teacher. She let me know that I did not have to cut little squares and sew them together. Roberta told me I could cut big chunks of fabric, I could do strip piecing, I could do it any way I wanted. She got me fired up.

How the Lunar Series Came About

I'd come home from teaching art and be shot. I didn't want to work on art work. Eventually I figured that if I was going to get the kids fired up, I would have to get myself fired up. That's when I started going to bed early so I could get up at 2 a.m. and start working on my own work. I'd work about three hours. That way I could get to school about 6:30 a.m. and let the kids come in early if they wanted. In the process I became really interested in the moon. Sometimes I would go out and get a coffee at the local place and come home, and every night the moon was different, different colors, different phases.

BLUE TRUNKS, 39" x 30", 2004

men and the art of QUILTMAKING ▶◀ JOE CUNNINGHAM

Quilters and Drawing

I have drawing in my quilt classes, and I tell the students that a line can be made by a thread or a pencil—either one. In England they just eat it up, they fill up my class before I get there. But here in the states, the minute I mention drawing in my class, people seem to be afraid of it; they don't sign up. Everybody is afraid to look silly or afraid to make a mistake. Most of the time a good original drawing by someone who is raw is better than one by someone who has taken a lot of drawing classes and become very tight—they are so refreshing. But people don't give themselves credit.

Working in a Series Part I

I can get inspired by color, by a shape, anything. Everybody gets stimulated to be creative in a different way. Most of the time if you look at the things right around you you'll find that *one something* that really stimulates you and gets you going. My art students used to think something was going to come in through the window and get them going. I get my ideas from working. That's why I love series: once I get one going it leads me to the next one. Sometimes I'll get three or four ideas coming out of just one. Usually your first shot at something is not necessarily your best. That's just the beginning, is the way I look at it.

Patterns

I never have used a pattern. I either just sketch it and go for it, or just go freelance.

Why Do This at All?

The greatest part of art is that it will make you a problem solver. Because every time you make a move you've got to make a decision about what your next move will be. Where you have a problem, who is going to solve it but you?

INFRASTRUCTURE No. 48, 76" x 58", 2009, detail below

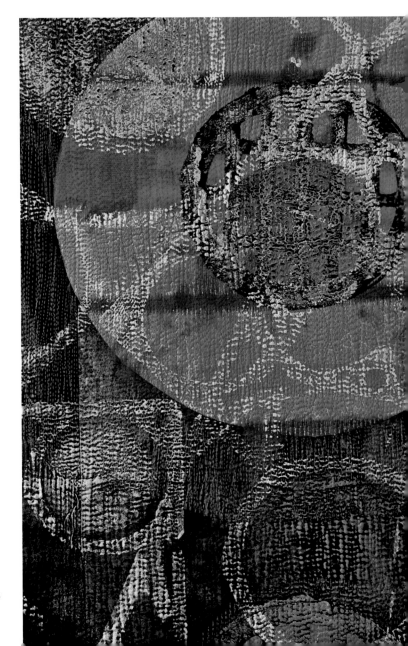

ROSE HAZE OF AUTUMN, 41" x 61", 2008

PHOTO: JAMES STICKLER

J. Phil Beaver

Self Teaching

I saw a piece or two in the 2000 Indiana Heritage show that used the bargello technique, a term I didn't know at that time. Trying to comprehend the bargello technique, I thought the pipes of a pipe organ would lend themselves to this technique I was trying to understand. I went with the pipes for my first two quilts.

Phil's Technique

After doing two bargello pieces, I was half cuckoo from all that precision cutting and piecing. I thought that if I do more of this precision work, my quilt career has just ended— enough is enough.

I knew how I wanted my work in quilting to appear, but the fabrics I needed didn't exist, at least not in the quilt shops where I shopped. And that's when I began painting my own fabrics.

If I were going away from piecing, I must be going to something that was not piecing. I had an idea I would build pieces, chickens, pumpkins, etc., from fabric I had painted, glue them together with tiny drops of glue to hold them together until I could get them quilted, build them up in layered ideas to get the images I wanted, pin all those layers together with 1,600 pins (for a large quilt), roll them up as a scroll and feed the layered work through a standard sewing machine for the quilting process.

LETTERS, 67" x 81", 2002 PHOTO: J. PHIL BEAVER

Why Phil Does This

I have spent a lifetime working in art and teaching art to others. When I retired in 2002, I was relieved that I no longer felt the need to work and think so hard. Now I am just having fun working in visual images, working in fabric and fiber designs. When people ask if I am thinking about light sources and things like that I tell them, No! I'm retired, I don't have to think about light sources anymore. It's been a lot of fun.

Painting the Background

Many ask, Do you paint your background fabrics? Or is everything you do a bunch of tiny pieces all cut up and appliquéd together? For ROSE HAZE OF AUTUMN the whole background is one big piece of fabric. I brushed the paint on to get the image you see.

Letters

For the letters in the LETTERS quilt, I began with white paper, tore it, creased it, wadded it, flattened it, watercolored around the edges, wrote the letters on the paper with black ink, and transferred the images onto white cotton fabric. They resemble paper letters that would come in the mail. Growing up in South Central Indiana, a few miles out of town and on a gravel road a quarter mile off the state road, we had no telephone. Living far from my mother's relatives, and with no telephone at home, you can imagine how important letters were. The mailman would come to our house about noon, drop the mail in our box, then head back out to the highway. If we had letters, Mom read them aloud. We could all read, of course, but it was better if Mom read them to us—a family thing.

SUNDAY AFTERNOON IN OCTOBER, 69" x 84", 2005, **detail right** PHOTO: J. PHIL BEAVER

CONNECTICUT SANITARY COMMISSION QUILT
50" x 84", 2009

Don Beld

No Stupid Questions

I took up needlepoint and cross-stitching in the 1970s as a stress management technique, but switched to quilting in 1992 when I took a 12-week class on traditional hand piecing and hand quilting techniques. I remember the teacher saying the first day, "There are no stupid questions; only stupid answers," but at the end of the class she looked at me with a smile and said, "Don, you proved me wrong; there are stupid questions."

The Cause

I am particularly drawn to 19th century reproduction fabrics and quilting patterns because I like the masculine colors of the 19th century and the geometric designs but also because I am an amateur history buff.

That connection with history has lead me to specialize in making what I call "historical" quilts and quilts that honor America's heroes.

I have a series of quilts that honor the casualties of 9-11, including one quilt, LET'S ROLL!, that is in the permanent collection at the Flight 93 National Memorial in Pennsylvania. I also made a quilt that honors the casualties from the terrorist at-

SAN JUAN CAPISTRANO, 96" x 96", 2007

tack in Madrid, Spain, that I call A Spanish Rose. I have also made quilts to honor Rosa Parks and one to honor Hillary Clinton. There is an old quilting tradition that honors American heroes and I try to do my bit in continuing this great idea into the 21st century.

Grassroots vs Non-Profit

In 2004, I began—along with my local quilting guild, Citrus Belt Quilters, Redlands, California—a national grassroots movement to make replica Civil War Union Soldiers' quilts for the families of the fallen heroes from the Iraq and Afghanistan conflicts. These quilts are based upon the six known surviving U.S. Sanitary Commission quilts from the Civil War and measure approximately 48 by 84 inches. I designed this movement to be grassroots,

not non-profit, because I wanted to honor the Community Service quilters who have made quilts continuously from the years before the Civil War to the present. Also, I wanted the families of the fallen to know that these quilts come from the hearts of the makers and express our sympathy and support to the hearts of the grieving family, rather than some "corporate" entity. We now have groups in all 50 states making these quilts.

Don's Studio in a Bag

One of the things I like about hand piecing and hand quilting is that they are mobile. You can take either with you wherever you go. When I was younger, I used to carry a gym bag because I was into running, biking, and exercising. Now that gym bag is filled with quilting supplies and unfinished blocks that I can take with me and work on while on planes, trains, and automobiles. ◄

FALLEN TIMBERS FROM THE ASHES, HEROES
78" x 78", 2008, detail right

A VALENTINE FOR ANN, 92" x 96", 1995

Jack **Brockette**

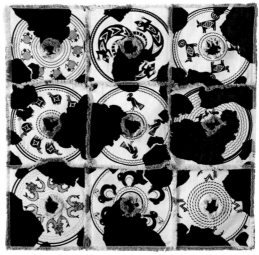

SACRED SPACES IX, 37" x 37", 1989

Hoop Skirts for Cows

When I was about nine, my Aunt Pebble took me to see *Brigadoon* with Nelson Eddy and Jeanette MacDonald. I was just so fascinated with the hoop skirts and dancing that I began raiding Aunt Nanny's and my grandmother's rag boxes, sneaking the fabric down to the barn and hiding it in the hayloft. After several weeks, my mother asked what I was doing since I was spending so much time in the barn. "Oh, we have three new litters of kittens in the hayloft and I am playing with them so they will not be wild," I said. Actually, I was spending my time trying to make hoop skirts. I was unwinding many bales of hay to have the wire to attach to it.

Around 3:30 one afternoon, I put out some extra feed for the cows and, of course, they all came running. I immediately locked their heads in the stall as if they were going to be milked again. Then, I dressed the cows for a fashion show of my creations.

DRAGONFLIES–RED/GREEN, 25" x 41", 2009

I pulled the newly created hoop skirts around their stomachs. I wrapped huge bows around their necks and attached flowers tied with strips of fabric to their horns. The sun was going down by the time all the cows were dressed. I was ready for my runway display. I opened the head slots and the cows immediately bolted out of the barn. They bolted and bucked out into the pasture by the road. I saw a car coming down the road—Oh no! It was my father and brother coming home for dinner. I got spanked, the cows stopped giving milk, and that was the end of my hayloft fashion designs.

When Did All This Start?

I was always aware of fiber. I did needlepoint and iron-on embroidery transfers when I was four and five years old. I wanted to be a fashion designer, but that was not something you could talk about in Texas at that time. I didn't have art in high school, but I was always the one who was asked to make the sign, or to do the drawing.

Jack's First Quilt

In 1980, I found photographs I had taken when I was a young banker in Dallas. I had returned to Dallas as Art Supervisor. I grouped all the pictures that had the word "Dallas" in them, such as Dallas City Limits, Dallas Playboy Club, Dallas Texas Bank—buildings, and signs, even policemen's badges. I took the photographs, made Kodalith® prints, and burned them into screens. (I have every one of the screens still.) Then I printed them. I used the Mobil Pegasus Flying Red Horse for the border of the quilt. Everything else was blue. I made it look like a cyanotype print. I silkscreened the red horse, and quilted all the white spaces.

Jack's First Quilt Class

In 1989 I received a call from the Silver City Museum members in Silver City, New Mexico, asking me to exhibit in the upcoming Mimbres-themed show about a tribe of Indians that flourished in A.D. 1000. I decided to make a quilt, so I went to Not Just Quiltz and asked for advice. My wife talked me into signing up for the block-a-week quilt sampler class. The first week, I made three blocks; the second week, I started playing with the patterns and redesigning them. Finally, I bought a bolt of black and white Holstein fabric and started making the quilt. From then on I made quilts all the time, quilts and jackets.

What's Jack Been Doing Lately?

Pojagi patchwork. I read about a woman named Chunghie Lee doing a workshop at the Split Rock Arts Program in Minneapolis, and I thought I would take a class with her. I was so turned on after that. I was determined to learn more about the technique. After I retired, I came up with a way to do the Pojagi seam on my BERNINA using a special foot. Now I can make four yards of Pojagi a day. I use it to make quilts and jackets, whatever I feel like.

RIGHT: DRAGONFLIES—BLUE/ORANGE, 31" x 38", 2009, detail

How to Get Started

When I got married I made a huppot (a canopy under which the Jewish marriage ceremony is performed), pieced it on the sewing machine and appliquéd it by hand. At the time I was making the huppot I was learning about quilting. I was quickly picking up the architectural necessities of how a quilt goes together. I would go into a quilt shop, a complete novice, and ask strategic questions like, "Why did you put the quilt stitches there?" But I never took a quilt class.

Sooner or Later You End Up Making Quilts

My work started out in a sort of folk art genre with appliquéd animals, the sorts of things I had done before with animals in fabric over wire. With my quilts, then, I would piece the base, then use the base to support the appliqué. So my first quilts were not patterned.

Goodbye, Frame

I taught myself how to hand quilt. I started with potholder-size pieces, just quilting in my hand to figure out how that worked. Since I didn't know how to bury the knot, I went into The City Quilter in New York and asked the woman at the counter how to bury the knot. She pulled a hoop out from under the counter and showed me how to bury the knot. That was all I needed to know.

Where to Get Fabric

I have an amazing fabric collection from the garment district in New York. I would get what was left over after they cut out the pattern at a couture house, so I have all these wonderful wools and silks.

Richard Caro

CORDUROY BASKET WEAVE VARIATION, 68" x 68", 2008

KING'S RANSOM, 72" x 72", 2009

16

men and the art of QUILTMAKING ▶▶◀ JOE CUNNINGHAM

Astrology and Quiltmaking

I had my chart read, the Eastern Astrology version, and it said, "You will primarily work with and be more comfortable with women." I took it to mean I might have a business partner who was a woman.

Studying Quilts

Two years ago I went to the International Quilt Study Center Symposium and it was amazing. Everyone was there. I don't understand why they don't have 5,000 people. In 2009, I presented a paper there on the QuiltGuy Yahoo group.

Bringing It All Together

My quilt work is all about the narrative surface. When I do my improvisational, freehand, pictorial piecing, I am not going to use templates and plan it out. I just have a sketch that I put up on the wall and I start piecing. Then I go in and hand quilt the whole piece. And that brings the whole thing together. ◗

VISION, 86" x 93", 2004, detail below

MY OWN FAULT, 69" x 84", 2007

Joe Cunningham

What I Liked About It Then

When I found the world of quilts in 1979, I felt like I had arrived at my true home. I could make beautiful things with my hands and I could study, write, and talk quilts and quilt history endlessly. Like music, it looked and felt to me like quilts could be the subject of lifelong study and practice.

What I Like About It Now

After 31 years, I feel like I am just getting started making the kinds of things I have dreamed of, and just beginning to understand quilt history.

How I Make Quilts

I start out with an idea of an action I want to perform, like cutting up some striped fabric and sewing it back together crazy. While I am cutting and sewing, something occurs to me that helps me understand what the quilt is about and how I am going to finish it. If I design the quilt first, I lose interest.

Hand vs Machine

Some quilts call for one kind of work, some for another. My most rewarding time in the studio is when I am quilting by hand. But I will do whatever it takes to follow the path where a project leads me.

What I Am Trying to Do Now

What I am trying to do is to make quilts that anyone could make, but that only I *would* make— quilts that are the result of everything I have seen, everything I have experienced, and everything I love to do.

SNAKE IN THE GARDEN, 73" x 73", 2000

About Joe Cunningham

I first "met" Joe through the quilting books he co-authored with Gwen Marston. My favorite is *Quilting with Style: Principles for Great Pattern Design*, American Quilter's Society, 1993. The homage paid there to the richness that the texture of hand quilting brings to a quilt top is pure Joe (and Gwen, but this is about Joe). Although Joe has developed a robust machine quilting enthusiasm, hand quilting helped establish his aesthetic sense and reputation and remains a big part of his repertoire.

Then I met Joe in person when he was teaching classes and performing his "Joe the Quilter" musical offering at the 2008 AQS Quilt Show and Contest in Des Moines, Iowa. Well before then I had decided that the next quilt book I most wanted to read was one about men who quilt. As the new executive book editor for AQS, I was suddenly in a position to make this book happen. Fortunately, Meredith Schroeder agreed with the idea, and wonder of wonders, so did Joe. He had been thinking about such a book, too. Good fortune that our paths crossed.

Who Joe Is

Joe will say that all you need to know about him is in the introduction to this book and on his Web site. I beg to differ. What you also need to know is that he embodies the word "genial," is rife with all manner of artistry, and is living proof that the briar patch does exist. If you have the chance to meet him, hear his lectures, enjoy his music, or take his classes, do so.

What Joe Has Done

Ultimately, Joe's contribution to quilting will be how he has integrated it into his whole life. He has embraced a notion, seized an opportunity, made the best use of available resources, forged a path, let go of stereotypes, celebrated differences, and generally pieced and embellished an extraordinary life in celebration of the layers of fabric held together by strands we call quilts. He has created some fine art

along the way. And he created this book, a first about men who quilt and his initial solo writing effort.

The patterns he offers here cover the waterfront from traditional to contemporary, patterned to improvisational, accessible to inspiring. Rather like Joe himself.

Andi Reynolds

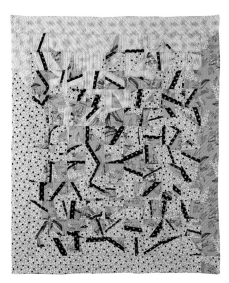

CUBIST ROSE, 58½" x 76½", 2009, detail below

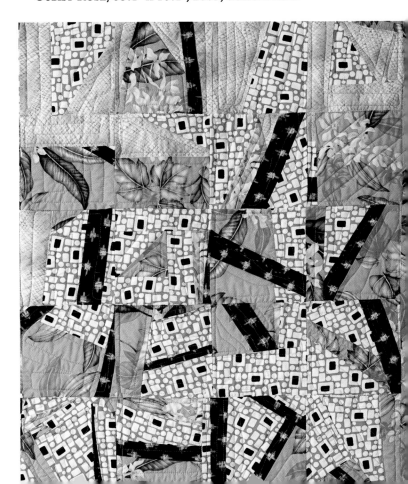

Earliest Sewing

My mother keeps telling me that I used to make doll clothes for my sisters when we were kids, but I don't remember that.

Doilies at Dockside

I was in the Navy for 10 years, then I was appointed a warrant officer in the Army. When I was in the military I taught myself how to crochet and that's what I did for a pastime. When I was in the Army I ran boats. We'd pull into the pier and I'd be sitting there after lunch and, just to have something to do with my hands, I would sit there and crochet doilies. When I quit smoking that was one thing that helped me keep from smoking anymore.

André Emmell

WONKY SQUARES, 104" x 104", **2009**

HELEN'S DIAMONDS, 56" x 71", **2009**

CRITTERS IN THE STARS, 48" x 48", **2007**

Why Make Quilts

About 15 years ago, when our twin granddaughters were born, I thought I would try to make quilts for them. So, I did. I had seen quilts and heard about people who made them, but I had never known anyone who did it. But I guess the idea of making something that personal for my grandchildren kind of got me started.

Studio/Doghouse

My wife says I've deserted her. I get up in the morning, come downstairs and make my coffee, then go upstairs and visit her for a while when I know she's up, and I don't go back up until lunchtime. I actually have a bedroom and a full bath off my studio. We call it "The Expensive Doghouse."

What He's Doing Out There

I jump around so much in my quilting. I'll do hand appliqué, then machine appliqué, then quilting and then piecing. Plus, I'm in a vintage exchange group. Twice a year we make sets of blocks and we exchange them to do reproduction quilts with 1800s' reproduction fabrics. I've got about 10 quilts here in the studio hanging on hangers, ready to be quilted, and I've got a design wall with quilts on both sides of it ready to be finished.

Andre's Designs

I always fall back on traditional piecing and/or appliqué. I had done a blue and white appliqué quilt for a friend's 25th anniversary. I entered it in the local quilt show and it won First Place and Best of Show, and that really turned me on.

Quilter Among Men

Any guys I talk to, when they ask me what I'm into, I'll say, "Well, my hobby is making quilts." And then the guys will look at me and want to start talking about sports. And I'll think, "Are you out of your mind? I'm about as interested in sports as donkeys flying." So I'll just roll my eyes and think, "That's where this conversation is going." Then I'll start talking to their wives.

BELOW: WONKY SQUARES, detail

FIVE POINT STAR, 84" x 84", 2007

John Flynn

PHOTO: CLARK MARREN

How John Got Started

My wife, Brooke, was learning to quilt and she decided that if I could build a bridge, then surely I could build a quilt frame. Apparently my first few models weren't acceptable. In my own defense I decided to prove that my quilt frames were actually functional; I started hand quilting her quilts. You know—"This is a perfectly good quilt frame and you should love this"—but the rhythm of hand quilting hooked me immediately. It's that intricate hand/eye coordination that just sets your mind free.

The Rewards of Hand Quilting

Everybody talks about hand quilting like it's going to be a painful operation. They just don't give it a chance. I sponsor the Merit Hand Quilting Award at the IQA Quilt Festival in Houston, a beautiful thing, but we struggle to get four or five entries a year. And we get the same four or five people entering each year. It is like with appliqué—fusing and gluing are designed to eliminate a part of the quiltmaking from which a lot of people get the same kind of feeling that I get out of hand quilting, and the main part of making one of those old Baltimore Album quilts is the process, not the end product. What happens is you have this thousand hours of pleasure and then at the end you've got this quilt.

How to Quilt

Quilting in a hoop is a real awkward thing. You're holding onto this thing while you're trying to quilt and turning it so you can quilt in one direction, which ruins the whole experience in my opinion. Then you end up with injuries or a carpal tunnel

SIGNS, 53" x 53", 2003

WAKAN KCI YU ZAPI SINA, 52" x 70", 2003

situation. The way I quilt, in all different directions using all my fingers, I can quilt 10 or 12 hours a day with no problem.

Thimbles

I use a plain old brass thimble. Initially I had a hard time finding a thimble that would work for me. I work off the side of the thimble, so a lot of these modern thimbles that are designed to work off the end don't work for me.

Sewing Machine Collection

I spent three or four years just hand quilting Brooke's quilts. I had no interest in sewing cloth together—I just wanted to do the fun part. Then I did some wholecloth work. But eventually I had to sew a little bit and then the sewing machine just fascinated me. In classes where everyone would bring a sewing machine I would run into all of these odd bobbin configurations. Something would always go wrong and I have a compulsion to fix things. So I started collecting machines for study. That was the start of my sewing machine collection.

Designing Quilts

I'm pretty traditional. I like to make combinations of traditional blocks. I've done that with a lot of blocks—Wedding Ring, Dresden Plate, and other traditional blocks—and engineered a lot of the problems out of them. The basic designs haven't changed in 100 years. What I consider a breakthrough for the Double Wedding Ring is instead of cutting all those wedge-shaped pieces, sew the strips together and sew a little dart here and there. This makes it possible for anyone to make it. You know, engineer some of that skill that's required out of it. The bridge business was no different. You have this pretty complex structure that you had to break down into steps so that any workman who walked in off the street without skills could put a bridge together. You have to break it down into extremely basic steps. I eliminated some of the skill required when I started laser-cutting the pieces for people.

RIGHT: FIVE POINT STAR, detail

Stars and Suns

I got interested in Native American designs and my Feathered Sun series of quilts are all sort of Sioux-influenced. I really got interested in the Star quilts and the giveaway quilts and all of that. Then the latest thing for me is the laser cut, like the Storm at Sea, Wheel of Mystery—repeating blocks so you can get a lot of patterns out of the same shapes.

Accurate Piecing and Pressing

Brooke's aunt wouldn't even glance at the front of a pieced block. She would just turn it over and look at the back. That sort of trained me that the back is pretty important. If you don't press the seams in the right direction you can't get a good result on the front. I try to focus on that when I am teaching how to piece a quilt—how to get all the seams to lie in the most natural way possible, because if you get a big pile-up of seams, your problems will continue.

What We Really Need

They've spent millions of dollars on the electronics for sewing machines and they still haven't got a laser-guided sewing machine to keep a consistent seam allowance. I don't understand why, since that's the one thing that we really need. ▱

The Lead Blanket

I made my first quilt when I was 14. I drew out a crazy quilt on cardboard pieces I used for templates. It has all these old fabrics from my grandma and my mom's stuff. I don't remember why I made it. It was 1978 and I was into all this Americana, back-to-the-land stuff. I had these old wool suiting samples. It's extremely heavy, like a lead blanket. I still have it.

The Child Connection

I didn't make another quilt for a long time. Then, at some point after I got married I decided it would be a good thing to make a quilt. The minute we moved out to the country my wife got pregnant and I ended up making a quilt for my first son. I tied that one. At that time, I didn't know how to quilt by hand.

Scott **Hansen**

TURKISH DELIGHT, 66" x 69", 2007

BASKET CASE No. 1, 48½" x 50½", 2009

THE M SISTERS TAKE SCOTT TO THE BOOKSTORE (BORDERS, THAT IS), 47" x 51½", 2008

The Retail Detail

In 1994 we went to a quilt show and I bought a fat quarter pack. Some time later, I bought the first issue of *Quilt Sampler*, the special edition from McCall's that features quilt shops. I had been in retail management for a while and I thought I wanted to open up a quilt shop, so I called every single person in that magazine—either wrote them a letter or called them.

What We Did

Instead of opening a quilt shop we decided we had to build a house for our family.

The Pattern Tester

I started going to the local quilting guild meetings. That was where I met Sara Nephew. I asked her, "How do you write quilt patterns?" And she said, "You want to test a pattern?" So I said yes, and I tested a pattern of hers called Hollow Cubes. After her book was published, she got a call from a magazine, and they wanted to publish that quilt (GARDEN BLOCKS) for their article. Then *Keepsake Quilting* picked my quilt to highlight the book in their catalogue. Then soon after that, Rocky Mountain Quilt Museum called and wanted to use it in one of their men's quilt shows.

Short Order Sewing

At Quilt Market, Marci Baker of Alicia's Attic took me around and introduced me to all these people at fabric companies, and I got the idea that if you made samples, these companies would give you free fabric. Later I remembered that I really liked the fabric at Free Spirit so I emailed Jeff Prescott. We talked a few times, then last fall he called me and said, "We just got these fabrics for Anna Maria Horner. Do you want to make a sample from them?" It was one week before the show. I did it, but I ended up tying the quilt for Market in Houston.

Sunlight and Shadow

I always tell my students, "Don't worry about color, look at the value. If you like the color, that's fine, but if the value's not there, it's going to just blah together. Remember the old saying, that value does all the work but color gets all the glory." 🖻

BELOW: THE M SISTERS TAKE SCOTT TO THE BOOKSTORE (BORDERS, THAT IS), detail

(MAN STUFF #1) HAMMER QUILT, 84" x 72", 2008

Luke Haynes

(AMERICAN NOSTALGIA #3) ABRAHAM LINCOLN
75" x 45", 2009

How Luke Got Started

My mom and I used to go yard sale-ing and we found a box of precut squares that seemed like something could be done with it. I was studying fine art at the time, and looked to one of my favorite artists, Chuck Close, and his process of using colored components to construct a whole image. So using my basic knowledge of sewing straight lines, I took the squares that I had and constructed a whole piece out of them.

Appliqué

All my work is machine appliquéd. Often I will draw with my sewing machine afterwards. I will just use thread to draw if something is smaller than a nickel, because it will take too much time to appliqué and my sewing machine is right there.

Size

I work in three different scales. One is pretty small, one about as big as I can handle, and the third is full-sized quilts that are nearly too large for my studio.

LEFT: (ON MY BED #2) COVER, 105" x 105", 2007

men and the art of QUILTMAKING ▸◂ JOE CUNNINGHAM

Wish I Had a Sylvia Plath

A friend of mine from high school went to Oxford and she came back after she got commissioned to do a play for a Sylvia Plath festival. She said, "I'd love for you to design the backdrop for it." It needed to be portable, because the play traveled to Paris, London, and Edinburgh. I designed it and we talked about it. The kitchen theme was very pertinent, and the window is a screen for projections. I went out and bought four or five different textures of white fabric—warm white, pure white, etc.,—cut them all to the size of square that I used, taped them to printer paper and ran them through my printer at home. I took them out and sewed them all together, then got someone with a longarm machine to help me quilt around some of the larger pieces. The play is called "Wish I Had a Sylvia Plath."

BELOW: (MAN STUFF #1) HAMMER QUILT, detail

Man Stuff

I've got a show in the works called "Man Stuff" where I've got quilts of a hammer, a big screwdriver, and a mounted elk's head—stuff like that. I get a lot of questions about being a quilter, because whenever I tell people what I do, you know, they will raise an eyebrow or dismiss it out of hand. Then when I show them pictures of what I do, it's a whole different world as soon as they see images of what I work with. So I wanted to play with that a little bit and say, hey—I'm still a male, I'm just doing something that is usually attributed to women. I can put a big picture of a Ducati on there.

Drawing and Quilts

My drawing instructor at Cooper Union said, "Every drawing you make teaches you how to draw your next drawing." I take that to heart. From everything I make I try to learn more about the craft and the process and the ideas and try to push it forward.

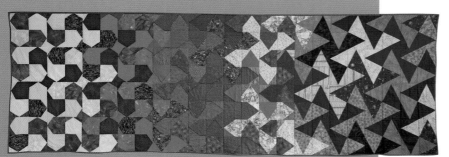

MARDI GRAS, 66¼" x 52¼", ©2007

Raymond K. Houston

PHOTO: SCOTT LOKITZ

I Dare You to Sew

I was in high school in Warrenton, Missouri, and I had a female classmate whose mother was a seamstress. She used to come to school and say, "My mother made this outfit and my mother made that." Nice cute outfits. This was in the late '60s. I got fed up with that. So one day I said, "Well, girl, anybody could do that!" And she said, "Well, let's see YOU do it, then." So I went to the library and read all about dressmaking and went to the store and got a pattern to make a shirt.

ESCHER! GESUNDHEIT!, 144" x 48", ©1999

Father and Son

I ended up doing all the sewing for my family—seven kids. Before the school year we would go window shopping and the kids would pick out the clothes they wanted. They would pick the fabric and I would pick the patterns and make all the clothes for everybody. My father was always standing off to the side saying, "I wonder what this means?" And of course it meant just what he thought.

Eventually, my father said, "That doesn't look all that difficult." And I said, "Well, sure. Get a pattern and get some fabric." He was wearing his favorite pattern—blue jeans. I showed him how to take them apart, iron the pieces flat and use them for a pattern, then sew them back together. That's how he learned how to sew. So, where most fathers and sons would bond over football, baseball, camping or fishing, we bonded over a sewing machine. When I left home he ended up doing all the sewing for the family. Now that he's retired, he sews a lot of quilt things for me.

LOLLOO/P4/II, 90" x 60", ©2006

American Quilt

In the summer of 1976 I decided to make a quilt, not because it was patriotic but because it was Americana. I got a book and taught myself to hand quilt just like I had taught myself to sew. I thought I would give that quilt to my parents for Christmas. And I did give it to them for Christmas, four years later! I said to myself, "Well, you're never going to do that again!" So I eventually taught myself machine quilting—pin-basting and quilting on my domestic machine.

Symmetry in Quilt Design

Once I read a book on symmetry, a math textbook (*Handbook of Regular Patterns: An Introduction to Symmetry in Two Dimensions,* by Peter S. Stevens, The MIT Press, 1981). It had nothing to do with quilts, but I realized it would be perfect for designing quilts. So I thought I would write a book on symmetry for quilters. Then I saw a book on symmetry by Ruth B. McDowell (*Symmetry: A Design System for Quiltmakers,* C&T, 1994), and another one by Jinny Beyer (*Designing Tessellations: The Secrets of Interlocking Patterns,* Contemporary Books, 1999). They did it first, but my system is different.

Quilt or Coverlet?

I use starch-stiffened muslin for foundation pieces and the muslin then becomes part of the quilt. Unlike paper piecing, you don't have to tear it out. But when I use these two-layer squares plus batting plus backing, it tends to make the quilt too heavy. These days I have taken to using flannel for the backing and no batting at all. That way I have three layers of fabric making up the quilt. It makes a lighter weight quilt you can use year-round—a year-round coverlet.

The Most Fabric

I am not a typical quilter in that I don't own a stash. I think that the person who dies with the most fabric is still dead.

Why Quilt?

I quilt because I enjoy quilting, because I feel I'm good at it, and because each quilt I make helps me learn something new.

BELOW: MARDI GRAS, detail

How Michael James Makes a Quilt

The way I've been working since 2002, my pieces develop both through planning and through spontaneous engagement with the materials and processes. Since I create all of the printed fabric that I use, I invest a fair amount of time in planning and developing those fabrics. This part is a bit more calculated and purposeful. Once I get the fabrics in my studio, I begin to play with them, usually without a fixed idea in my head of what the end result will look like. I don't do a lot of sketching, although I will make simple diagrams to work out size and scale problems. I like to get the fabric on my studio wall and then enter into a dialogue with it. I do something, then I step back and take in what's there. I listen for the work to respond, and then I respond in turn. It's a dialogue, and if I'm really listening the result is usually a work that reveals a certain rightness and integrity. At least that's the goal.++

PHOTO: JUDITH JAMES

Michael James*

PHOTO: LARRY GAWEL

A SYSTEM OF CLASSIFICATION, 48½" x 56", 2009

PHOTO: LARRY GAWEL

GRID WITH A COLORFUL PAST, 47" x 36", 2008

PHOTO: DAVID CARAS

REHOBOTH MEANDER: QUILT #150
53" x 53½", 1993

men and the art of QUILTMAKING ►►◄ JOE CUNNINGHAM

How He Felt After His First Trip to a Museum at Age 15

The thing that I remember most is feeling—going there—feeling like I was coming home, feeling like this was where I was supposed to be, feeling some sort of affirmation, I guess. I can say this in retrospect more clearly, but at the time I don't think I fully understood what I was feeling, but it was significant and it was something that confirmed for me that art was what I should be doing.

On Choosing to Work in Fabric

No other material is so closely connected to the human body. And I think that essential quality is what gave me a rationale for adopting it as an expressive medium, because I felt that anything that was so closely connected, so necessary for human functioning, had value, a kind of essential value that, to me, legitimized it as an artist's material, as a material at least with potential creative value.

Why Quilts Instead of Paintings?

The materials require a different form of manipulation, and you either connect to one form or another. I connected better to the processes of sewing than I connected to the processes of taking a stick and dipping it in paint and applying the paint with the end of the stick, or with some other tool, to a board or canvas.

Does Being a Man Help?

The fact that I am a man has its advantages, because as an anomaly you get noticed. And so in that sense I think being a man in this field initially drew more attention than being a woman might have, although—and I've always said this, and I maintain this to this day—that the quality of the work is ultimately the determining factor, and if the work hadn't been good, the fact that I was a man would not have been enough to give me a career. ▨

*All quotes from *oral history interview by David Lyon with Michael James, 2003, Jan 4-5, Archives of American Art, Smithsonian Institution* unless otherwise noted.

++How Michael James creates fabric and makes quilts comes from his *Creative Statement, January, 2009*.

BELOW: Grid with a Colorful Past, detail
PHOTO: Larry Gawel

STARLIT NIGHT, 50¾" x 55¾", 2008

Michael Kashey

LUCKY THIRTEEN, 65½" x 64½", 2006

BAROQUE FUGUE, 40" x 40", 2008

When Did This All Start?

As far back as I can remember, I've always been fascinated by textiles. Since I was three or four years old, I remember being intrigued while watching others do needlework. As a youngster, I pursued this interest at the local library and taught myself how to knit, crochet, tat, and embroider, etc.

Learning Needlework

In the '40s and '50s when I was growing up, men were closeted needleworkers. As a growing child, I was not only interested in needlework but in the creative process. It wasn't until my early twenties, that I openly practiced my craft. As a public school art teacher, I taught all forms of art to my students. To my surprise, many boys enjoyed working with fibers and textiles.

The TV Quilt Connection

In 2000, I saw Elly Sienkiewicz demonstrate Baltimore Album quilt techniques on Alex Anderson's *Simply Quilts*, television program, and I decided that I wanted to design my own version of a bride's quilt. Thus appeared WHAT'S IN A NAME: ROSE WINDOW TREE (page 102). Simultaneously I was designing my second quilt, THESE ARE A FEW OF MY FAVORITE THINGS, which also depicts fond memories (page 69).

Two Quilts a Year

I'm working on my 21st quilt. My quilts are very tedious, time-consuming, and mostly handmade. I am in no hurry and am not interested in cranking them out. A one-inch square could take me an hour or longer. The more intricate, the more I like it. It's something that just pleases me.

What's Not to Like?

I like the formality of radial design. There is something fascinating in how the wedges fit together to form interesting secondary patterns. I like the whole process from designing, cutting, sewing, sandwiching, to quilting. I like the idea of planning as I go. All of my life I've been trained to design a piece thoroughly before I make it, but now I enjoy being more spontaneous while creating and am often surprised with the end result. I let it speak to me. Wherever the spirit leads me, I like to let it flow, as opposed to coming up with an idea and sticking to it.

Care for a Pattern?

I could never select a pattern from a magazine or book and say, "I am going to make *that* quilt." I would be bored stiff if I had to make 50 or 60 blocks of the same pattern.

Philosophy of Visual Life

Having completed my third degree in art, a masters of fine arts degree (MFA) in textiles, I find myself focused in the direction of quilt design and construction. Choosing not to succumb to the fast-paced, technological world, I am stimulated to seek solutions to quilt design ideas. Using various needleworking techniques and processes, my quest is to create a unique piece—the more intricate and challenging, the better.

RIGHT: STARLIT NIGHT, detail

UNPIECED, 48½" x 56", 2006

CATHEDRAL NOTRE-DAME, 14" x 14½", 2009

Alan Kelchner

PHOTO: SEARS PHOTOGRAPHY

Alan Has Done It

I've been doing needlework all my life. If it takes a needle or a hook or a shuttle, I do it. I've done knitting, crochet, bobbin lace, embroidery—you name it.

Thanks, Grandma

The first quilting thing I ever did was in 1976. During the Bicentennial I lived in a small town and somebody thought it would be a good idea to bring my grandmother up on stage and demonstrate how to quilt at the celebration. After the demonstration they brought the quilt frame to our house and set it up. And Grandma taught me how to quilt.

My Big Mouth

I didn't quilt again for 10 years. Then a coworker's mother died and left an unquilted top. She wanted to find someone who could quilt it and I said, "Oh, I can do that!" So my first experience in quilts was a paying job.

Restoring Enthusiasm

I was making traditional quilts and getting bored—how many squares can you put together?—when I moved to Jacksonville, Florida. There I found a *Quilters Newsletter* magazine issue and learned that people were fixing up old quilts like I was and making money at it. So for about five years I did that. Through someone else I found a client and she asked me, "Can you fix this early 1800s quilt?" and I said, "Yes, I can do that." Then I looked at my partner and said, "What have I done?" I got the quilt in the mail, fixed it, and sent it back. Just like that.

Paper Brush Rags

I keep trying to go into different directions. On the FREDERICK quilt, (page 69), except for his picture, the whole thing is made out of paper towels. They were my brush rags.

Quilt It Three Times

My cathedral series started out as photo transfers on fabric. I just painted the fabric with acrylic medium, then slapped the print down there and rubbed real hard. I did that just to get the general shape of the cathedral, then I went back in there with my pastels. They are all raw-edged. I just glued everything together. There are three layers of quilting on it. First I followed the edge of the fabric, sewing all the way across the piece. Those little crisscross lines happened when I just wondered what would happen if you just sewed a bit, hit the reverse and twisted it, and nudged it in a little different direction. Then I did a monofilament meander all over it.

How to Handle Rejection

I have a completely clear quilt. I went to the fabric store and they had some scrap box vinyl. Then it came to me that I could use three layers of it, layer it with some gold tulle in the middle, and then quilt it with monofilament for top and bottom threads. It got rejected from the Visions show. When I got the rejection letter, I just said, "Oh, well. Someday I'll be in Visions. You'll see."

Freedom

I'm not troubled by whether it's art or not. Sometimes I make quilts, sometimes I make art. I know what I'm doing. ⬛

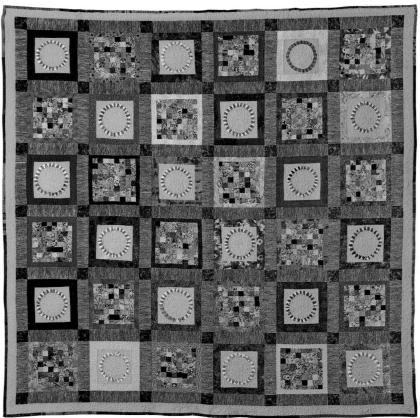

RECTISPHERE, 84" x 84", 2005, **detail below**

Life Changing Moments

What got me into this whole machine quilting thing was that back in 1997 I spent a year making an appliqué quilt top and somebody was telling me about this machine quilting stuff where you could send your top off to have it quilted. And I sent it off to this lady, and when I got it back, it had been quilted entirely in monofilament thread. I was just livid. And I realized I had never thought to question the thread or anything. Then I thought, "Okay, I could do this." I had heard about Linda Taylor. Her shop was just up the street from me. So I went up there and watched her for about two or three hours and asked a few questions. I asked Linda, "How much is one of these machines?" She told me. Then I went across the street to the

Richard Larson

PHOTO: NICOLE DICKINSON

EARTH STAR, 84" x 105", 2004

ANGELS GATE, 59" x 84", 2000

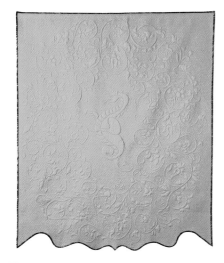

ELIZABETHAN WOODS, 62" x 77", 2006

men and the art of QUILTMAKING ▶◄ JOE CUNNINGHAM

bank and I said, "I want to buy a quilting machine. This is how much it is. Will you loan me the money and use the machine for collateral?" And they said yes. So I bought a machine without even trying it.

What Business Plan?

I was a corporate travel agent, but I started getting these quilt tops in from these lady friends of my mom up in Burkburnett, Texas, and that's how I got my practice. Pretty soon people started hearing that I had this quilting machine at my house and I was doing quilting and I started getting more and more quilt tops in. I ended up making more money doing that than sitting behind a desk.

So I took a leap of faith, quit my full-time job, and began the machine quilting business. Then I got a call from a quilt shop owner who said, "Would you be interested in putting your machine in my shop? I won't charge you any rent. You can do all of your machine quilting here, and all I will ask is for you to quilt my class samples for free." I was happy to do that and get my machine out of my house. Especially because I was always a little worried about women going to a man's house to drop their quilts off, because who is this guy? And is this safe? And it might be kind of uncomfortable. And that is where I got a lot of my exposure, at that shop. Then the shop closed and I moved over to another one, and then that one closed. I thought, this is ridiculous. So I finally got my own space and bought another machine.

Who Runs the Machine?

I've got two longarm machines, but I don't have a stitch regulator on either machine. Everything I do is all me.

RIGHT: ELIZABETHAN WOODS, detail

Custom vs Panto

Custom work is my reputation. Edge to edge is my bread and butter. I don't nickel and dime people, I do what I say I'm going to do and I run it as a business. My backlog runs three to four months for custom quilting. I still do the pantograph patterns because if there is some person who is just beginning, I want to make sure that they can have a finished quilt without it costing a lot of money. Plus, it gets them hooked!

NOSHI, 66" x 73", 1997

Don Linn

Forced to Quilt

As a result of a corporate downsizing I needed a job, so I bluffed my way into upholstery and furniture repair. I only had one customer, and my wife, Donna, dragged me to a quilt show. I didn't see anything, I just walked through to pacify my wife. Then I saw this lady running a quilting machine in the vendor area, and stood there and watched her for a while. I love machinery. Finally I worked up the courage to ask her what she was doing, and she took me by the arm, dragged me through the show, and made me really look at everything. A month later I ordered a longarm.

Driven to Design

I did everything backwards in this

OUT OF AFRICA, 48" x 58", 2005

SWAHILI MAIDEN, 41" x 31", 2006

business. I started out being a longarm quilter, not knowing anything about quilts or quilting. Then I decided after a few years that I needed to have some of my own quilts to send around to shows, so I had to make something of my own. I made a very simple pieced design, but it was a challenge for me, never having done it before.

Quilting Is a Lonely Job

Being a longarm quilter is a lonely job. You need to like being by yourself. I don't quilt for people anymore, so I'm doing more designing and teaching classes, which I find more enjoyable.

Questions People Ask

One of the questions I get a lot from men is, "How do you put up with the women?" But what stands out to me is that I love to make things. And I love to be around people who are creative. If I could find a group of men who were creating as I can see the women are, I would probably hang around with them. But so many men will do something like just going out and playing golf. I have nothing against that, but at the end of the day you have nothing to show for it. And I just prefer being around people who are creating things.

The Art Quilt Takes Over

When I started the only thing I had to study and learn from were books on antique quilts and traditional designs, and I made up my mind that those were the kind of quilting designs I wanted to do. The manufacturer I bought my machine from assured me that it would do all that, but it wouldn't, so I had to redesign and rebuild the machine to do what I wanted. It was all traditional at the time. Now I am seeing a lot more art quilts than traditional.

How to Get Famous

One time I was working away in my hovel of a

RIGHT: NOSHI, **detail**

studio—no heating, no air conditioning, listening to a baseball game—and I heard Bob Uecker refer to himself as "Mr. Baseball," and I thought, 'If he can be Mr. Baseball, why can't I be Mr. Quilt?' It was a joke on myself, something to make a little fun for my friends. Then my wife and daughter bought personalized license plates for me. And about that same time I was asked to be the featured artist at a show for the local guild here in Redding, California. The local paper did an article on me and took a picture of that license plate, and unbeknownst to me, that article was rerun all over the country. Because of that I ended up on *Simply Quilts*. Then I came up with this trunk show where I put on an old time medicine show for quilters, and the name just stuck. Now I do this entire trunk show wearing a top hat and tuxedo, and I get people up to help me and I never know what's going to happen. Nobody goes to sleep during one of my shows.

What He's Trying to Do

I look at myself as three things: part educator, part entertainer, and part motivator. And at the guilds it should be entertainment. I want them to forget about their problems for an hour. ▣

How to Iron

When I was growing up in Pittsburgh we had my great-grandmother's White treadle sewing machine in the cellar, and I was forbidden to touch it, which of course meant that touching it was all I wanted to do. I would take ripped up rags and cut them out and I would sew on that machine, sneaking it, until my grandmother finally showed me how to work it and how to load the bobbin. There was nothing for me to sew so I used to make clothes for the neighborhood kids' Barbie® dolls. I made clothes for Troll dolls, and I would put on Troll shows. One Christmas my father got me a Vac-U-Form® machine to make plastic cars and trucks with. I got rid of all the plastic and used the hot plate for a dry-cleaning presser to iron my doll clothes on.

Mark Lipinski

WINTERBERRY, 111⅜" x 111⅜", 2007

BLUE SKY THROUGH AUTUMN LEAVES, 99" x 99", 2007

CRYSTALS, 75½" x 75½", 2008

men and the art of QUILTMAKING ▶◀ JOE CUNNINGHAM

Quilting Time

I adopted my son from South America and I was supposed to be in Paraguay for two weeks, but when I got there he was very sick; I needed to stay longer and I got caught in this coup and ended up being there for six months. My plan was to come back to the U.S. and resume my job as executive producer for Lifetime Television, but I decided my son and I needed some bonding time, so I quit my job to stay home with him for a year.

One day I came upon the Eleanor Burns quilt show on TV and thought, "Oh, you can't be serious," and I watched it as a joke. Coming from being an Emmy Award-winning producer, it was so strange to see something obviously produced on a shoestring without the sort of production values I was used to. Well, the next day I tuned in again, just for a laugh. And then the next day and the next, and pretty soon I was hooked. I thought, "Oh, I could do that." So I went out and bought *Quilts! Quilts!! Quilts!!!: The Complete Guide to Quiltmaking* by Diana McClun and Laura Nownes, a rotary cutter, and a mat and taught myself how to make a quilt top. It had three perfect corners and one that looked like the map of Italy.

What Mark Is Good At

I'm not the best quilter, I'm not the best designer, I'm not the best anything. I'm the best spender, and I have to have every new object. That's what I do best. When my friend got a Grace hoop and started talking about how wonderful it was, I knew I had to have one, too. She let me borrow it. I'll tell you what, if you start out your career as a TV producer you probably are anal retentive and if you didn't start out that way you end up that way. So it was important to me to get 4,835 stitches per inch and I drove myself crazy with it. I finally took a class with Kaffe Fassett and learned how to do big stitch quilting. Now I enjoy it. But I send most of my quilts out to be quilted.

RIGHT: **CRYSTALS, detail**

Opposites Attract

In my opinion, opposites attract. I don't mean that in terms of sexuality, but just a sort of natural attraction. For instance, I have always liked my female teachers more than I liked my male teachers. And coming from a daytime TV background, I learned a long time ago to think like a woman.

A Leg Up

No matter how far we have come as a society, I feel kind of sad sometimes because women are still expected to play this really good girl type of role, where men are not constricted by that type of thing. So for a man to come into the quilt world and start a magazine and get noticed, it is easier. From my third quilt on, everything has been published.

What He Was Trying to Do

I think what I have brought to the table is this: my goal has always been to quilt guilt free, to have fun with it. If you don't like it when you are done, throw it away. If you have a quarter-inch seam, great. If it's a one-eighteenth-of-an-inch seam and it has held together, great. It's about letting go of all the fear, the anxiety about being in front of the sewing machine. It's about discovering who you are through that needle and thread, and about letting go of that fear of failure.

JAVA JUNCTION, 69" x 88", 2008

Mike **McNamara**

PHOTO: GARY EMERSON HART

QUILT FOR AN OHIO POET, 64" x 84", 2008

Mac's First Sewing Machine

I made my first quilt in 1976. My mom then asked her mom if I could have Auntie Vee's sewing machine.

"Of course you can have that old machine," she said, "for eighty dollars." She was a great politician, not such a great grandmother.

Who Changed His Life

My friend Ann Schroeder (an inspirational Cape Breton quiltmaker) told me there was a course we should take with a woman named Nancy Crow. We took that two-week course at Haystack* in 1994 and it was an eye opener. At Haystack you are allowed to go in any time of the day and work on your stuff, so I pulled some 24-hour days. Prior to that I would have made quilts by way of graph paper—Pinwheels and Log Cabins, that sort of thing. But once I took that quilting course at Haystack, I really had a lot of fun doing curved piecing and I just took off and did my own version of all that.

Decoding His Quilts

When I make my quilts they are so saturated with personal significance to the recipient that they really are like inside jokes. I see a lot of people looking at my quilts and, since they don't know about that person, they don't know what the pig means, or what Elvis is doing up there, or why I incorporate tires in my quilts.

* Haystack Mountain School of Crafts is an international craft school located in Deer Isle, Maine.

men and the art of QUILTMAKING ►◄ JOE CUNNINGHAM

Working Alone

I work alone. It is so much easier to not let people know I am making them a quilt and then to surprise them with it. It is like someone telling an artist how to paint. I love the sense of freedom in working alone. I just don't want to get into measuring and making each block the same and so on.

How He Wants It to Look

The way I make a quilt is that it is for someone, it is for fun, it says something about them, and the style is simple. I go to the mentality of who it is for. And I go for an even distribution of lights and darks. And I also hope that it looks like a kid could have done it.

Confidence

From the very first quilt I made, I said, "I can make one of these things."

VERMONT/NEW HAMPSHIRE, 51" x 81", 2009,
detail right

Jim's First Frame

When I was five or six years old there was a house sale up the hill and I had a dollar to spend. At the sale I spotted a large wooden thing that was selling for a dollar, and I didn't know what it was, just that it was a large wooden thing and it was a dollar. At home I found out it was a quilting frame, and I just stored it in my parent's garage for many years. After visiting a church group, I got it out, installed a top in the frame with a batting and backing, and started quilting. The year was 1973. I've been quilting ever since.

Non-Rocking Stitch

I tried the rocking stitch that the ladies at the church used, but I quilt differently than that. I push in the first stitch and I pull it back to where I want it, then I push up with my bottom finger and measure it. I can get four or five stitches on my needle at a time before pulling the thread all the way through. I'm so satisfied with hand quilting that there is no reason for me to go to the machine. I quilt every

Jim Mikula

CHRISTMAS – 2009, 90" x 108", 2009

day, sometimes 10 or 15 hours a day. I always have things lined up to quilt. Usually I have quilts of my own that are ready to go, too.

Quilting vs Teaching

I taught theater and English in high school for 30 years, from 1968 to 1998, and quilting was my after-school therapy. Instead of strangling some kid

RED LOG CABIN, 94" x 115", 2003

at school I would come home and quilt for eight hours. Quilting is quiet time. I go into my own little universe, a meditative state where I come up with all the solutions to everything. Solutions to all the problems in the world. And all the things I should be doing, but I would rather be quilting.

Quilting in a Big Way

Sometimes I hand quilt almost excessively. I won't go somewhere because I'm almost done with a quilt and I'm going to sit here and finish it. I like to do the big ones. The old frames I have are 100 inches wide, and now I have a new set of boards that are 120 inches wide. So I can quilt up to about a 110 inches.

What He's Doing Now

I've always gone back to three-dimensional things like Tumbling Blocks, so I might go back to something like that if I run out of things to do. My next commission is for a non-profit that puts up a big Christmas display every year. They have commissioned me to make a pictorial kind of quilt of their display so they can raffle that off. I try to draw the whole thing first, then go through my fabric and see what I can fit where, then go and buy the extra stuff I'll need.

What Else Jim Does

I do lots of local theater, directing, choreographing, and acting.

AMERICAN BEAUTY URNS, 85" x 101", 2005, detail right

A GREAT WHITE WAVE, 86" x 105", 2005

M Mueller

Bathmat Inspiration

What inspired me was that when my wife, Georgie, got her job in the library at Appalachian State University and we moved to Boone, North Carolina all our stuff was in storage; I had no writing studio and I had no creative outlet. At Christmas time Georgie asked me what I was going to get her, and I told her I had been thinking about getting her one of those little tables you could eat dinner on while you watched TV. She said, "No. I want you to make me something." And I had just finished sewing up some new upholstery with my grandmother's old White sewing machine for a piece of furniture I had repaired. So I had some upholstery fabric sitting around and I decided to make a quilted bathmat out of it. We ended up hanging it on the wall.

The Book

That year we went to a New Year's party where Georgie took my quilted piece for show and tell, and my friend Susan Jones said, "You need to come and visit me in Asheville. There's a book I want you to see." So I went to visit Susan and she brought out the Gee's Bend book (*The Quilts of Gee's Bend: Masterpieces from a Lost Place* by William Arnett and others, Tinwood Books, 2002). I realized in the first few pages that I was looking at a highly sophisticated aesthetic based on improvisation that took delight in things not lining up and such. In the hour that I looked at that book I got permission to go ahead and do what I wanted to do. That was the first aesthetic I followed, not the fussy Anglo/European idea, but the idea of, "Hey, take what you've got and make something beautiful out of it."

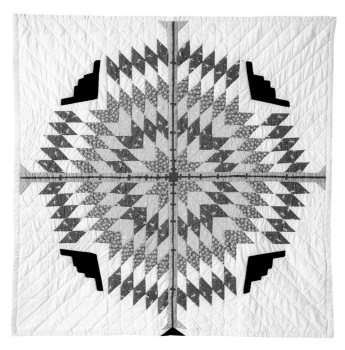

...UNTO ME, 49" x 49", 2005

The Pattern Factor

There's something in me that cannot take a pattern and see it through to the bitter end. At that point the quilt dies. I try to keep it alive in all my quilts by playing with things so they never resolve.

Sometimes Yes, Sometimes No

Remodeling my house I was very careful to incorporate and preserve symmetry wherever it was appropriate. As a carpenter you want standardization throughout the project, throughout the house. But then when it comes to quilts, the side of my brain that kicks in is the narrative side rather than the craftsman side. So even though I may make a plan in the cutting and the laying out of the pieces, it is more like writing a short story; I can fill it in and if there is a narrative element that kicks that outline awry, I can go with the new narrative element.

What to Do with Them

All of my quilts are standard bed-size pieces. And there is something about being able to say, should worse comes to worse, it's a quilt and you can always use it to keep warm. That's really necessary for me.

PEARL AND BEN'S WEDDING QUILT, 87" x 105", 2009, detail right

Does It Matter?

I don't really feel like my gender plays much of a role in my quiltmaking. I saw an old book about Appalachian quilters, and there were a few men in there who made quilts. I know that in parts of Africa men make the textiles and I know enough about the older English tradition to know that tailors used to make a lot of quilts. So I don't feel particularly transgressive at all. ▱

AUTUMN COMES TO DELECTABLE MOUNTAINS, 82" x 82", 2003

Scott **Murkin**

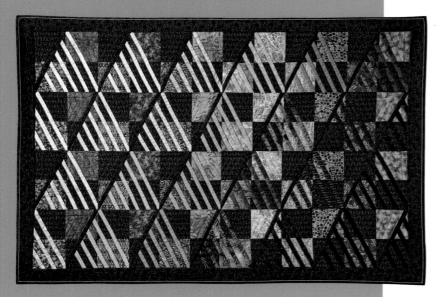

OVERLAY IV: JUNGLE LIGHT, 52" x 36", 2008

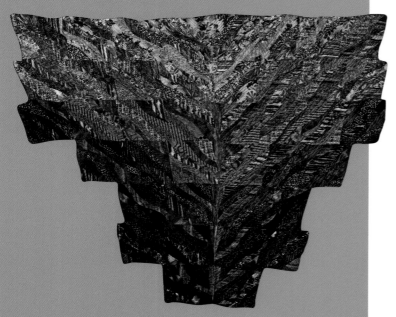

STRATA XXVIII: OPEN PIT MINE, 66" x 53", 2007

Getting in the Zone

Even when you come home tired and say, "I'm just going to sit down and do a few pieces," before you know it 45 minutes or an hour has gone by. You just kind of get lost in it.

Why Quilt History Is Important

There was a two- or three-year phase where I had to hunt down all the really rare antique quilt books. I don't have many pattern books, but I have all the history books, all the art books, and all the design books. From the beginning it felt very natural to know where we came from and where you fit in the whole big picture. I think it makes me a better quilter to know where all that came from. So I went through that really intense phase of collecting all those books and reading them all and assimilating all that information. If you went to art school you would do the same thing; the first thing they would teach you is everything that went before.

Tradition vs Innovation

Historic quilters were really innovative. People talk about traditional quilts as if they were always traditional, but at one point Log Cabin was the new thing. I go through phases where I tell myself, "You really need to choose [between art quilts and traditional quilts] and then I just tell myself, 'Just shut up,' because I'm not going to."

How Scott Plans a Quilt

For my early quilts, I would draw designs on graph paper by hand, photocopy them, and color them seven different ways with pencils before I got Electric Quilt® software. I've kept every piece of design paper that I've ever generated and as you look through my files, with the early ones there will be a whole folder for each quilt. Now all the paper for a whole quilt will be maybe a Post-it® note with a little scribble on it. And for a bunch of the quilts, no paper exists.

Favorite Technique

One of my favorite techniques is free-form curved piecing, where I just lay pieces down and cut them freehand with a rotary cutter and sew them back together and just keep doing that in different variations until I'm happy with it. I'm on number 57 in my STRATA series. Sometimes it's literal layers and sometimes it's the illusion of layers, but just building those layers upon layers really speaks to me.

Scott's Favorite Part

The quilting design is my primary focus in quilting. I have a talk I do for guilds called "Quilt As Desired" where I talk about figuring out how to listen to your quilt top tell you how it should be quilted. The change in texture from the piece being three things to being one thing absolutely captures me every single time. I love when you find the perfect design that will make everything sing.

On Running Out of Ideas

I have so many ideas that have gotten left by the wayside because by the time I got to them I was already beyond that point. I can't make them as fast as I can think them up.

RIGHT: AUTUMN COMES TO DELECTABLE MOUNTAINS, detail

Planning vs Spontaneous Sewing

It just depends on the design. Sometimes you need things to fit together in a certain way and you need to know the measurements in order to get them to work that way, and other times you don't. It's the same thing with quilting designs. Some designs I need to mark in order to get them to do what I need them to do, and other designs I don't. And the number that I don't have to mark has increased over the years.

Being a Man in a Quilt Guild

About the third guild meeting I attended, one of the guild members who is closer to my age came over to me and said, "So, why do you make quilts?" She tried to say it offhand, but it was clear this was an important question, and I was very uncertain what the correct answer was. So I went with the KISS principle—Keep It Simple, Stupid—and I said, "Well, I just really like fabric." And she said, "Oh, I really like fabric too!" and that was it: I was in.

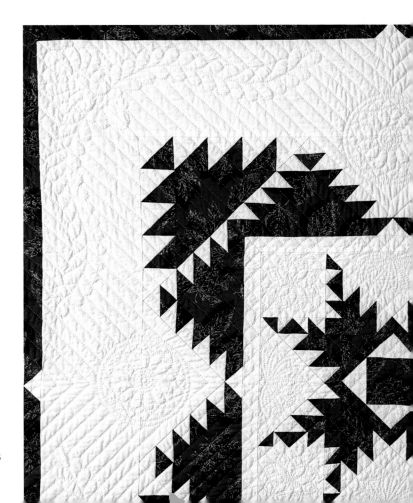

Fashion vs Quilts

I went to the Art Institute of Pittsburgh because I wanted to be Calvin Klein, but to be a fashion designer you have to learn how to sew, and I had no desire to do that. Instead, I trained to be a video editor. So it was not until my stepmom bought a quilt at a thrift shop when I was in my early 30s that I even saw a quilt. I got really turned on by the fabric designs from the forties and fifties and also the idea that it was an early form of recycling. I got so into it that my stepmom looked in the *Pennysaver* and bought me an old Singer® 201 sewing machine.

TV as Quilt School

I learned a lot from watching all those sewing shows on PBS. I might think, 'Well, I don't want to make that,' but I still learned a technique or got an idea of how to do something.

Shawn's Double Batting and Backing

I've been just pinning everything down and then sewing it down with invisible thread. Then I'll just go over everything and stipple it with invisible thread. Then I'll add another batting and another backing and then I'll go back with different colored threads and I'll quilt it again. That makes a very stiff quilt. So they hang real nice and they have this really great texture. I like that effect.

Shawn Quinlan

PHOTO: SHAWN QUINLAN

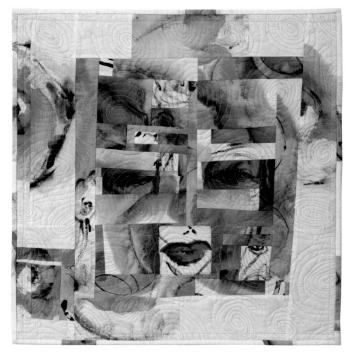

PINK LADY, 19" x 18", 2002

Pattern or Image?

It would drive me crazy to just make a repeated block pattern. I can start out with just an idea, maybe just an interesting fabric. I love all the steps. It took me a long time to learn to love all the steps, because I used to hate to do the binding, used to hate certain steps. Now I'll spend a month or two on the design wall just on the designing, then when I know that's done I get to relax and do the appliqué, appliquéing everything down and then the quilting of it...so I like the whole process. And it is therapy, too.

Quilter at an Art Show

I'm always going to art shows and museums. And at first I was afraid of being too derivative of

NO ESCAPE, 80" x 43", 2009

somebody else's work. But now I just try to make it my own, and it seems to be working. When I'm doing an art show I'll be the only quilter who is standing there, and I get a lot of attention. So I was really lucky that way. I'm still really excited about getting my quilts out there and getting all these reactions. Having this big stash of fabric and exploring all this stuff is really great. It took me a long time to find my niche, to find my art form, and I'm sticking with it.

On the Content

I'm kind of like a fortune teller. When I look back on some of my early stuff about money and greed and hypocrisy, which is something that is hard to portray through art, I see that there are a lot of things that get my goat. But you have to have some humor in there, too. People always want to know what does that mean? or what are you trying to say? and I want to say, just take it loosely.

The Joy of Modern Machines

Four or five years ago I bought a BERNINA, and I love it. After you use the leg lift and the needle down, you have to wonder how you worked before. There is something about the machine—working with it. I really like the sewing machine and how it can force all these pieces together. ▣

Falwell Quilt, 39" x 47", 2006, detail right

Men in History

I think a lot of men made quilts in the closet for a long time. Then just a few gave license to the many. One of the stories Paul Pilgrim and I found when we were curating *Gatherings: America's Quilt Heritage,* American Quilter's Society, 1995, (funded by the Lila Acheson Wallace Reader's Digest Fund) was about a man in the Midwest who used to make quilts using the lap quilt method. When he was working on one of his quilts he would position his chair so that, if anyone came in unexpectedly, he could duck it behind him so they wouldn't see what he was doing.

Technique to Me

One thing we learn from quilt history is engineers and other men with technical jobs often got involved in quiltmaking. But I am not someone interested in the mechanics or technology of it, or fine, fine stitching. I got into quilts because first, as a collector, I thought it was important to be able to make a quilt to better understand the process. Then, as a painter, I found that it was just another vocabulary or medium of expression.

Color Career

I did my undergraduate studies at Worcester Art Museum School, Worcester, Massachusetts, during the time when Joseph Albers was the head of Yale's Art and Architecture department. Interaction of color was an extremely important part of my education at the time. My whole artistic career has primarily been through that kind of influence, and the study of close values rather than contrast has always been my interest. The first time I saw an Amish quilt I thought it was an Albers painting hanging on a line.

Gerald **Roy**

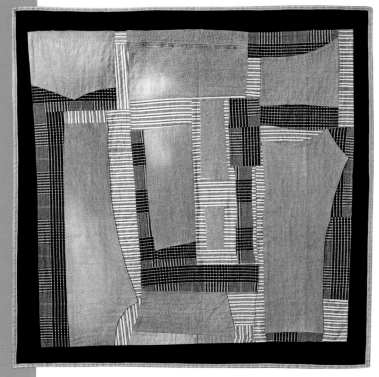

WINDOWS & WHARFS PROVINCETOWN, 46" x 49", 2009 COLLECTION OF: ELEANOR & STEPHEN SCORE, BOSTON/ PROVINCETOWN, MA

FRIENDS, 38" x 46", 2010

men and the art of QUILTMAKING ►•◄ JOE CUNNINGHAM

How to Use a Featherweight

When Paul was ill, he told me, "Before I die, I want to teach you how to use the sewing machine, because I think you are eventually going to want to make quilts with the machine." So in the last couple of years of his life he showed me all that I needed to know about machine sewing, which is not a lot. I use a Featherweight that goes forward and backward.

Cutting and Rhythm

I've collected a lot of early homespun, mattress ticking, old denims and jeans—things with mends and all kinds of repairs. Those are the fabrics I am working with today. Usually I cut them and make units to compose with. I will even set up a rhythm with the rotary cutter, repeating the same motion, almost like the rhythm of following a piece of music, or conducting. I find that if I can develop a rhythm and then suddenly cut in that same way, I end up with all these related shapes, but none of them are exactly the same. I will sew a series of those and then combine them, playing with them until I end up with a composition I find challenging.

Why Make Quilts?

My own experience has made me realize that for the old-time quilters it would have been a lot easier to go out and buy a blanket than to put this time and energy into making a quilt, unless they were getting something else out of it. And what they were getting out of it was pleasure from the creative process—the whole satisfaction of cutting something up and sewing it back together in a new and unique form. The time and energy you had to take to do that must have given them some relief from the drudgery of everyday life. It was a significant source of pleasure as evidenced by the results. It is a never ending challenge and pleasure for me.

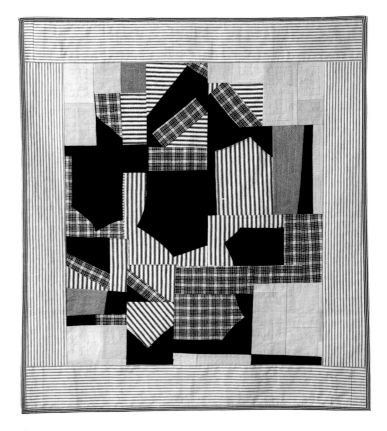

SHADOWS, 40" x 47", 2009

RIGHT: SHADOWS, detail

AIR SHOW, 81" x 81", 1992
COLLECTION OF: THE NATIONAL QUILT MUSEUM, PADUCAH, KY

Jonathan **Shannon**

How Jonathan Started Making Quilts

Jeffery and I bought a country house in Sonoma, California, and in that house was a stack of Americana magazines that had been left behind. I was looking through them, and there on the cover of one of them was a beautiful quilt. And I thought, 'Now, wouldn't it be nice to make one of those for this house.' My intention was to make a traditional quilt. So I went to the local quilt shop and bought copies of *American Quilter* magazine and what was then *Quilters Newsletter Magazine*. Well, I went home and I discovered that quilting was a lot more than just these antique quilts.

Jonathan Discovers the Quilt World

As soon as I heard about it I joined the San Francisco Quilters Guild, and then the East Bay Heritage Quilters, and it immediately put me in contact with what was happening in the quiltmaking world, not the art quilt world. I was the only man I knew involved in quilting, and I felt—and still feel—quite role-model-y about that. And I was also a very openly gay man who had a partner who came to every meeting with me because I didn't drive. And I enjoyed the fact that I was so openly accepted and welcomed within that circle. So I thought my being a man was important; that, in a way, I was making a path.

AMIGOS MUERTOS, 89" x 89", 1994

PHOTO: SHARON RISEDORPH

RED, 77" x 77", 1995

54

men and the art of QUILTMAKING ▶◄ JOE CUNNINGHAM

First Ribbons

Six or eight months after I started making quilts I entered two quilts in the San Francisco Quilters Guild show and won first prize in both categories.

Quilting As Competition

After my quilt won third place at the first AQS show I entered, and the quilt was featured on the cover of *American Quilter* magazine, boy, my competitive juices were just flowing! So I took a National Quilting Association class on quilt judging from Katy Christopherson, thinking that I wanted to know what was considered "good." I wanted to know what the top people thought was important in terms of a prize-winning quilt. That was the year that Caryl Bryer Fallert's quilt CORONA II: SOLAR ECLIPSE won Best of Show at AQS, the first machine-made quilt that had ever won. And our little judging workshop was abuzz...a machine-made quilt won Best of Show...should it or shouldn't it? This event sparked a lot of ideas for all of us about how open a judge had to be to new ideas. That it couldn't just be stitches per inch. It couldn't just be sharp points. That those things were important when the quiltmaker thought they were important.

A Man's World

When AIR SHOW won Best of Show at AQS I stood in front of it for three days and talked to quilters from all over the world. What was especially interesting was that a lot of husbands came up to me and said, "You know, when I look at this quilt I really begin to understand what my wife has been doing all these years." And I thought, "Yes! That is exactly what I wanted it to do." That is why I was glad to be a male quiltmaker, to have brought it to the attention of so many people that a man could make quilts, a man could make good, personal artistic quilts, and at the same time quilts that had a place within the quilting community, and were accepted by that community.

RIGHT: AIR SHOW, **detail**

A New Kind of Quilt

After AMIGOS MUERTOS I thought I had done everything I had set out to do with quilts. I didn't need to win again. So I thought about what I had loved about quiltmaking, and that was that I really loved the textiles, the fabric. And what I had done so far was to take a piece of textile and cut it to the point where it was no longer particularly distinguishable as its innate self and use it to make a picture of something else. What I wanted to do next was to use interesting textiles in a way that explored what they really were. This led to the series of those large crazy quilts with pieces of textile in large enough chunks where you could see that it was a piece of Japanese woodblock indigo, you could see that it was a woven Guatemalan, that it was a piece of antique chintz. ▰

George Siciliano

Make It Yourself

My wife, Virginia, had been quilting for well over 35 years. Now understand Virginia would do just about anything for me, so perhaps I caught her a little off balance in 1997 when I said about a Lesly-Claire Greenberg quilt in a book, "Hey honey, this is a really cool looking quilt. Would you make it for me TODAY?" She said, "If you like it so much MAKE IT YOURSELF." So I ended up getting my own fabric and made my first quilt.

Competitive Juice

Virginia hand quilted several of my earlier quilts. I made a large quilt and while she was quilting it a friend saw it and suggested we enter it in the guild quilt show. This would require guild membership. She finally convinced us to join, we entered the quilt and it received several ribbons, including a first place blue.

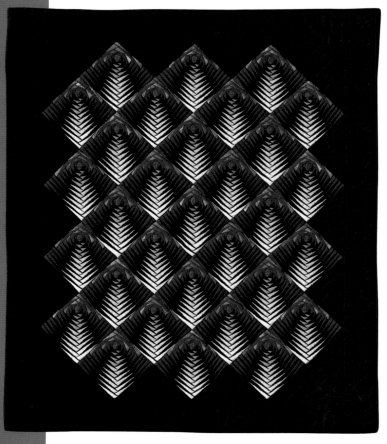

TREE DIMENSIONAL, 14½" x 17", 2001

ILLUSIONS, 11" x 11", 2008
COLLECTION OF: THE NATIONAL QUILT MUSEUM, PADUCAH, KY

SOIL FESTIVITIES, 11¼" x 11¼", 2002

men and the art of QUILTMAKING ▶◀ JOE CUNNINGHAM

Why Go Small

After I had made several wallhangings (but only two bed quilts) my wife "retired" as my "in house quilter" (a position I created just for her), so I started machine quilting my projects. The small yoke on these home sewing machines makes machine quilting quite impossible (for me). As I was not making "bedding" but wall art, I decided to see just how small I could go. My first miniature quilt was AUTUMN MOSAIC. It's 11" square and has over 2,200 pieces.

Perfection

I compete in shows all over the world and I'm very particular about my workmanship. If I sew in a piece and I do not like it, it comes out. A tiny error in a miniature quilt sticks out like a sore thumb. I tell my students, even if you're making a quilt for a baby who will do things on it we do not talk about in polite company, it's still your work, so make it right.

How Small Can You Go

When talking about miniature quilts, size really does matter. I'm restricted as to size by, of all things, the needle. I want to make a quilt with over 3,000 pieces where the blocks would be ¾" square or less. I could use silk to reduce bulk but the stitches must be very, very small, and with the needles currently available on the market, I would destroy the foundation before I finished the block. I need a really thin needle.

What I've Been Doing

Over the last 10 years I have been developing a "Triple Duty Seam Allowance Guide" to help in foundation piecing. I designed it for a left- or right-handed quilter and it creates a ¼" or ⅛" seam guide. We currently have a "patent pending" on this tool.

Paducah First Place

So there I was, sitting in the awards ceremony audience at the 2008 AQS Paducah show. I sat in the middle of the row as I knew I would not get an award. This was confirmed when I saw the 2nd and 3rd place quilts; they were magnificent. I was staring up at the screen and my quilt ILLUSIONS came on the screen. I just sat there looking at the screen. They announced my name but there I sat. Finally, Ginny elbowed me in the ribs and said, "You won stupid, go get your award." As I worked my way to the aisle I kissed every woman I passed. The only one I missed was MY WIFE! We had some conversation about that.

The Difference

Virginia has a quilt in The National Quilt Museum. Of course, I have two in the museum, but who's counting! We've given our workshops and presentations to at least 50,000 folks over the last 10 years and NOBODY, not one person, has ever asked Virginia how she started quilting, yet it's the first question they ask me. Most people feel that it is strange to have a man sewing, yet many of the greatest tailors are men. I explain that I'm simply an artist and I use fabric as my medium.

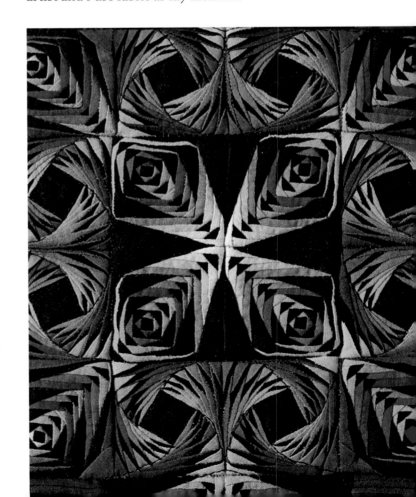

RIGHT: SOIL FESTIVITIES, **detail**

David Taylor

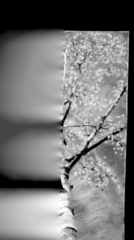

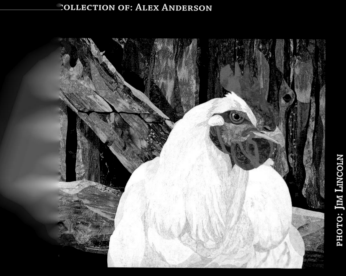

SALLY AT THE WINDOW, 40" x 51", 2006
COLLECTION OF: ALEX ANDERSON

PHOTO: JIM LINCOLN

I AIN'T NO SPRING CHICKEN, 57" x 39", 2007
PRIVATE COLLECTION

PHOTO: JIM LINCOLN

Pre-quilt Stash

In 1992 I shipped 23 cartons of fabric with me when I moved to Steamboat Springs, Colorado, from Florida. I always had this thing in the back of my head where I would say, "Some day I'm going to make something out of this." I grew up the first 35 years of my life buying fabric and not knowing why I was buying it. I would just see prints and think, "I've got to have this fabric because someday I'll make something out of it."

Collecting and Using Fabric

My studio has taken over my whole apartment. I've got my Handi Quilter® in there, and my BERNINA, and eight feet of shelving for fabric, four feet of shelving for hundreds and hundreds of fat quarters. I mostly work with one-of-a-kind, hand-dyed, hand-

A YEAR UNDER THE ASPENS, 95" x 40", 2008
PHOTO: DAVID TAYLOR

made fabrics. I do buy commercial fabrics, but I love using another artist's work in my work, because it's a collaboration with somebody who designed those thread colors, with somebody who designed that fabric. And so you're using all those other artists' work in your piece. My work is only possible because of those artists doing their art.

What I Learned at Quilt Shows

I didn't have a clue. I had learned how to machine appliqué, I had learned how to choose fabric, I had learned how to make a binding. I started doing all this stuff I said I would never do. I went to the quilt show in Houston and some other major shows and I realized I had no idea—and I saw Hollis Chatelain, Caryl Bryer Fallert, and others whose work I just loved, and it made me think, "I could do this. This is what I'm supposed to be doing."

How to Get Started

I can't start a piece until I have all the fabric. Usually I have the idea and then I have to find the fabric. I start a pile of fabrics and I think, 'This is the next project.' But I would hate it if I ran out of fabric. So I make sure I amass hundreds of choices for that piece, and when I know I have enough, then I can start building it. The nearest quilt shop is 90 minutes away.

A Long Five Days

I'm a horrible student. I've only taken two classes, one with Noriko Endo, and one with Hollis Chatelain (her dye-painting class). In the first 20 minutes of that five-day class I knew that I didn't want to do that. And at the time she said, "Everybody can look at David's and see how NOT to do this." Of course, I did it my own way and it came out great. We've since become great friends. ◗

RIGHT: SALLY AT THE WINDOW, **detail**
PHOTO: JIM LINCOLN

BOHEMIAN RHAPSODY, 83" x 83", 2002

Ricky Tims

DAD'S LONESTAR, 93" x 93", 2001

TANGO, 64" x 66", 2002

The Olde Sewing Machine

Quilting found me in 1991 while I was working in St. Louis, Missouri, as a freelance music producer. My Granny Newsom, an 83-year old widow living in Texas, was proposed to by an 87-year old man named Pete whom she had known for decades but had not seen nor spoken to for several years. Granny immediately accepted his proposal and they were married two weeks later. When she moved to be with him, I inherited her old Kenmore® electric sewing machine.

Having the machine sparked my curiosity about sewing and I decided to make a Western-style shirt. Someone had told me that shirts were difficult to make so I rethought my decision and instead, decided to make a quilt. No one ever told me that making a quilt was difficult! In June I bought a beginner's quilting book that had instructions for a 20-block sampler and taught myself following the instructions. That first quilt was made using the technique of cutting and using templates from cereal boxes and then drawing around a template for each piece with a ballpoint pen. At that stage I didn't know rotary cutters existed. Each block was supposed to be 12 inches finished. My blocks varied from 11 to 13 inches and it is a wonder that I ever got the quilt to fit together. By the fall of 1991 I had learned about a quilt guild in my area and started attending meetings—learning a lot and making quilt friends. The rest is history.

men and the art of QUILTMAKING ▶◀ JOE CUNNINGHAM

Quilting + Music

Quilting was slowly invading my career as a conductor, composer, and producer. The decision to pursue quilting as a profession would never have been made if music had been deleted from the equation. I am fortunate to have found a way to use both music and quilting in a unique way. I am fulfilled because each has the ability to feed the other. It is a blessing to be able to do both and call it my profession. However, if anyone asked me what I wanted to do when I grew up, quilting would not have been at the bottom of the list—it would not have even made the list!

How It Feels

When I attended my first quilt meeting, I was timid and felt a little bit awkward. However, the ladies welcomed me with open arms. They were willing to share their tips and insights and encouraged me to keep on going. I did feel a need to prove myself. There's no doubt that when I took a quilt to a show-and-tell, it was scrutinized, but that was good for me. It drove me to excellence. I wanted to learn all the rules—and I did—but now I break a lot of rules, keeping workmanship at the top of my list.

My quilting techniques are very recognizable even if they are contemporary or unorthodox. I think that is what has helped me to gain the respect of these wonderful ladies. I stopped thinking about the gender issue a long time ago. I have become part of a community of quilters, creative individuals, people who have good days and bad days, those who celebrate victories and grieve losses, artisans whose well-spring of inspiration is sometimes full and sometimes dry. So ask me again, 'How do I feel being a man in a field dominated by women?' I feel accepted, respected, privileged, honored, blessed, and lucky to be a part of the incredible worldwide quilting community.

RIGHT: BOHEMIAN RHAPSODY, **detail**
PHOTO: GREGORY CASE

Father and Son

My dad started quilting the same week that I started quilting. Neither of us knew the other had started a quilt. That was very serendipitous, and quite spooky, to be honest. My dad has continued to make quilts all these years. Once, when he wanted to make a Lone Star quilt with all the diamonds, I said, "If, you'll make the star then I'll make all the inset bits and do the appliqué around the border." So we made this father-and-son quilt, which in itself became a novelty. DAD'S LONESTAR has ended up winning many prizes. Dad is now 81 and sews every day. This past year he has made about 12 king-size quilts. ◢

How to Start Teaching Quilts

Around 1970 I got a job teaching needlework for the local recreation center. One day I got a call from the director; she asked me if I knew anything about quilting and I said yes. I was working downtown near all the museums, so I went to the Jonathan Holstein and Gail Vanderhoof quilt exhibit. Some members of the National Quilting Association were in the lobby demonstrating quilting, so I explained that I needed to teach quilting but I didn't know how to teach it. So one of them, who just happened to be the president, gave me an outline for an 8-week course on the Nine-Patch.

How to Start a Quilt Career

In 1978 Hazel Carter gave a talk to my quilt group in West Virginia about how to organize a quilt group. We got talking and she asked me if I would organize the vendors for the first Continental Quilting Congress. Then, since I

Holice Turnbow

MORNING STAR, 24" x 24", 1993

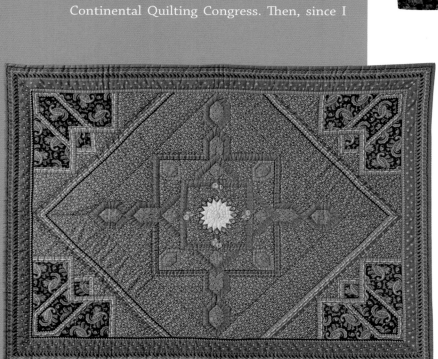

ORIENTAL RUG, 60" x 40", 1979

had been playing Ben Franklin in a local theater production of *1776*, she asked me if I would come out on stage each day as Benjamin Franklin and do the announcements. I still meet people to this day who remember that.

Postage Stamps and Baskets

I got a call from the U.S. Postal Service looking for a quilter from West Virginia because they were going to issue a stamp from there. Since the subject was baskets, I was asked to curate a quilt show, so I issued a call for Basket pattern quilts and Postage Stamp quilts. The Postal Service let me see the design of the stamp and gave me permission to work with one of the quilt co-ops in West Virginia. They made a block of the stamp pattern and they put a sheet of the stamps on the back and sold it on the first day of issue.

How to Start Another Career, I

In the 1980s I started to get invitations from all over to go around and teach. In 1985 my daughter was offered a job selling stencils for a company in Canada. Then I started designing stencils for them and started hitting the quilt show circuit. At one of the shows in the early 1990s a guy came around and asked, "Is it possible to print a large quilting design on fabric?" I told him it could be done if he had the technology, and he said he had the technology and asked me if I would design a line of wholecloth quilts for him. It was by copying some wholecloth quilt designs, redrawing them for different size beds, that I really learned how to draw quilting designs.

How to Start Another Career, II

One day I called the Smithsonian and asked them if they would be interested in licensing our wholecloth quilt designs. I worked with photographs of their wholecloth quilts, and they issued a series of six quilts called the American Collection. From then I started teaching quilting designs instead of patchwork.

How to Bind a Quilt

I spend a lot of time making crib quilts for the hospital. In the last year I have made over 200 wholecloth quilts, machine quilted, but then I bind them by hand. I started making these to analyze my own bindings to see what I was doing wrong, but then I became addicted to them. Now I sit at home in the evenings and do the handwork on the bindings.

The First Men's Group

I've started a men's quilt group here. It's not a guild, just a quilting bee. At my local quilt shop they kept telling me that this man had dropped in, that man had dropped in. So I sent a notice to the local newspaper and they came out and interviewed me for a story. I ended up with about 14 names. I try to start each meeting with about 20 or 30 minutes on standard stuff, like piecing or appliqué. It's near Sturbridge, Massachusetts, but we have people coming from Boston, Lowell, and all around. ▪

RAINBOW DAHLIA, 40" x 40", 2009, detail left

SUNSHINE AND SHADOW (DIPTYCH),
24" x 11¼" (each piece), 2004

David Walker

Fiber to Fiber

I made my first quilt in 1981. At the time I was still teaching school (I taught 7th grade for 22 years) and I was a weaver. I took a class and made a quilted pillow top. That's how it started. My first art quilt was in 1983 or '84.

Grade-A Faculty

I took a bunch of classes in the beginning, not knowing anything at all about quilts. If I had known how important these people were I probably wouldn't have done it. My first year I took a class with Jan Myers-Newbury. The next year I took three week-long workshops in a row. I took classes with Nancy Halpern for five days, Michael James for five days, and Nancy Crow for five days. I didn't have any notion of becoming an artist at the time. I just wanted to take these classes.

Straight from the Fabric

I did everything from scratch without an idea; I never drew them out. I didn't know how to draw, even. So I would always just start with the fabric. I didn't take a class on how to do the Ohio Star, for instance, so I never learned the rules or how to make regular blocks. I learned how to make blocks from Nancy Crow.

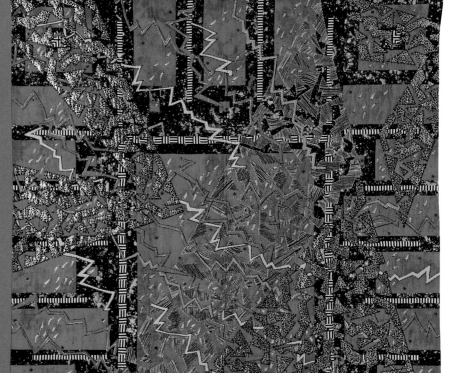

THE OTHER SIDE OF SILENCE, 71" x 98", 1989

A Sea of Women

I was the only man I knew for many years in the quilt world, but I was also the only man where I taught, because I was teaching at a Catholic school with nuns for my bosses. So I was always comfortable being around women.

The Men-only Shows

I've always refused to be in an all-male quilt exhibition. What are we trying to prove by separating ourselves? So when I started teaching quilting in 1990, I often got the impression that students thought my quilts were better because I was a man, although I never encouraged that at all. But that is why I never entered the shows. I didn't like the thought that my art work was being appreciated because I was a man.

Improvising the Quilt

From 1995 on all of my works were small. In my class an exercise I did which was very popular was that the students would sit around me for an hour or an hour and a half, and I would make one of these pieces from scratch. I would take out my scrap fabrics, and I would have my ironing board right next to me and I would have music playing. It was like theater, really. And I would make something from scratch, and they were always amazed that I didn't have that idea 45 minutes earlier.

What David Taught

In my teaching I didn't teach people so much about how to make their quilts, but about how to approach their lives. A lot of us self-taught artists have never felt confident about being artists, like we don't have the right to be artists because we don't have the degree. And that's what I taught, that you didn't have to have this degree to create art. Since most of the people that I taught were not formally trained, we were all in the same place. So we all ended up commiserating with each other. ▣

RIGHT: CHILD'S PLAY, detail

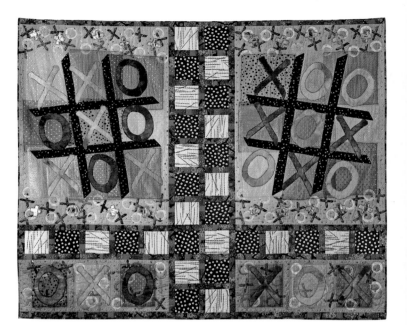

CHILD'S PLAY, 78" x 91", 1996

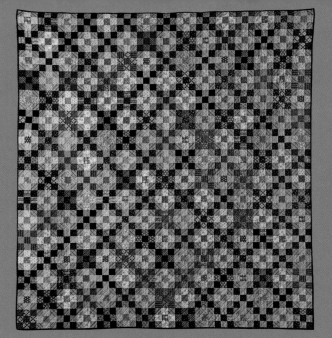

DOGWOOD, 85" x 94", 2009

Erick **Wolfmeyer**
PHOTO: ERICK WOLFMEYER

HOME SWEET HOME, 60" x 73", 1998

From Quilt Show to Quilts

In 1998 I just happened to be in Sisters, Oregon, the week after their annual outdoor quilt show. I had always been interested in quilting, but knew nothing about it at the time. I had a notion to make a quilt for the newborn child of the friends with whom I was vacationing. So I bought my first pattern and made my first fabric selections at the Stitchin' Post quilt shop. My then-partner David was well-versed in sewing and had a machine. He taught me the basics and within a few months, I had the paper-pieced quilt complete, including my own hand-quilting.

Unsung Quilters

Twelve years later, people frequently ask me how I learned to quilt. I tell them I still feel like I don't really know how to sew, but that I learned mostly through the kindness of many fellow quilters and shop owners. Today, by way of an intermediary in Elkhart County, Indiana, I collaborate with individual Amish women to do my hand-quilting. According to tradition, they decline personal recognition for their work.

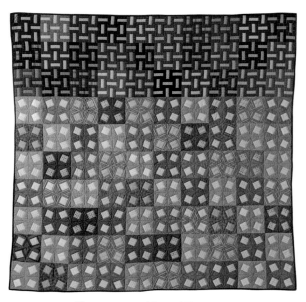

KIRICHIGAE, 87" x 87", 2009

men and the art of QUILTMAKING ▶◄ JOE CUNNINGHAM

Let the Borders Go

Since my work is usually heavily pieced, I rarely use borders, and the hand-quilting becomes mostly a function of utility. I am always amazed when I get a piece back from my quilters. They bring the work to life. I begrudgingly add the binding myself, but each stitch reminds me what I also love about doing it—the sense of accomplishment and resolution.

Beginner's Luck

HOME SWEET HOME is the second quilt I made while living in northern California. It set a precedent of creating my own patterns. Though it may appear appliquéd, it is based on the tumbling block pattern and paper-pieced with 16 different tessellating herringbone parallelograms. Most of my work, even the most unconventional, springs from longstanding quilt traditions. My BFA in photography from Washington University in St. Louis may help explain how I went from never having sewn to creating something like this. I made it as a social criticism of urban sprawl and the erosion of community. It would foreshadow the housing crash that came ten years later.

Inspiration

With early influence from writers like Thoreau and Loren Eiseley, my quilts express kinship to the world around me. I find inspiration everywhere— horizon lines, crashing waves, old farm buildings, birds in flight, Bible stories, game boards, even beer packaging—all of which I interpret as abstract expressions in fabric. My inspiration link is one of the most popular features of my website.

Pieces

Inasmuch as I am a product of everything that has come before me, so are my quilts. Like the women to whom quilts gave a voice long before society at-large, quilts have been my saving grace as an outsider. I was adopted by loving parents at seven months old. I arrived with a few stuffed toys, some medicine, and a note from my mother. Separated from my tribe, I have subsequently felt like a stranger in a strange land all my life. Quilting is my attempt to put the pieces back together.

Quilts are a perfect metaphor for a life well-lived. They require from their maker vision, initiative, adaptability, stamina, faith, and a finish-line focus. In return, quilts give far more than they require—beauty, warmth, purpose, affirmation, and most of all, forgiveness. ◖

RIGHT: KIRICHIGAE, **detail**

JULY, 91" x 103", 1991. Made by Jonathan Shannon.

THE GALLERY

ABOVE: SCHOOL FIGURES, 35" x 51", 1991. Made by John Flynn.

LEFT TOP: FREDERICK, 8½" x 25", 2009. Made by Alan Kelchner.

LEFT BOTTOM: THESE ARE A FEW OF MY FAVORITE THINGS, 67" x 84", 2006. Made by Michael Kashey.

ABOVE: **GRAMPS**, 70" x 60", **2006**. Made by Shawn Quinlan. PHOTO: SHAWN QUINLAN

LEFT: **QUEEN'S CROWN**, 40" x 40", **1998**. Made by Holice Turnbow.

OPPOSITE TOP: **UP THE STREAM OF GOOD INTENTIONS**, 72" x 72", **2010**. Made by Joe Cunningham.

OPPOSITE LEFT: **DRAGONFLIES – YELLOW/PURPLE**, 25" x 45", **2009**. Made by Jack Brockette.

OPPOSITE RIGHT: **DOUBLE WEDDING RING #1**, 58" x 80", **1996**. Made by Mike McNamara.

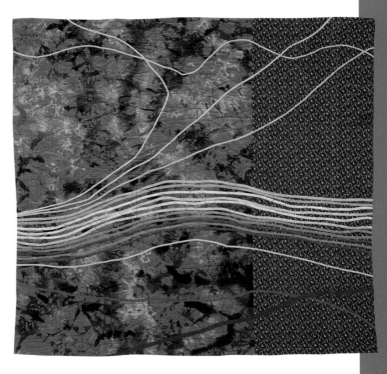

ABOVE: FT. HOOD MEMORIAL QUILT, 56" x 86", 2009.
Made by Don Beld.

LEFT TOP: MODEL AT REST: RED/ORANGE, detail, 39"
x 51", 2000. Made by Bob Adams.
PHOTO: BOB ADAMS

LEFT BOTTOM: DUSK A L'ORANGE, 13" x 13", 2010.
Made by George Siciliano. PHOTO: GEORGE SICILIANO

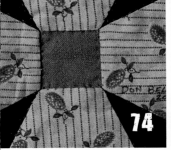

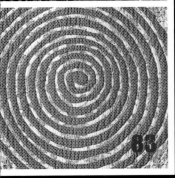

THE PATTERNS

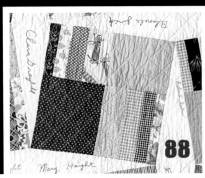

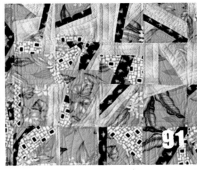

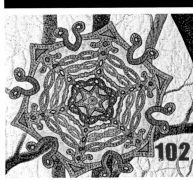

Don **Beld**

GREEK CROSS, 10" x 10", 2010. Made by Don Beld.

men and the art of QUILTMAKING ▶◂ JOE CUNNINGHAM

GREEK CROSS
Don Beld

Learn the Technique for Making 19th Century Potholder Quilts

Templates A – E (page 76) will make one 10" x 10" bound GREEK CROSS block ready to assemble into a Potholder quilt with other blocks or to display or use on its own.

During the mid-19th century (1840-70), a group or community quilt project affectionately known as Potholder quilts was extremely popular. Made of individually pieced, quilted and bound blocks (potholders), they were the ideal project for women to make as community service quilts in a quick and easy way. Of the six known Sanitary Commission Civil War soldiers' quilts, four were made in this fashion.

Piece the block by hand or machine following the assembly diagram. You can join the pieces in any order but you will have one or more set-in (Y) seams.

Layer the pieced block with batting and back fabric and pin or baste as preferred. The most authentic 19th-century batting available is Mountain Mist® Blue Ribbon 100% cotton. Traditionally, the back fabric would be pieces of fabric that the quilter didn't like or no longer needed.

Quilt the individual block either by hand or machine. Although machine quilting and piecing were uncommon during the Civil War, several of the surviving Civil War soldiers' quilts have blocks that are machine pieced and/or machine quilted.

Bind the quilted block with ¼" binding to match the seam allowance (cutting your binding fabric 1¼" inches will allow you to comfortably do this). The binding would NOT be double folded as in today's technique, but simply added by sewing down the seam allowance using a running stitch a quarter of an inch on the top of the block and then folding over and using a half-fold under to sew to the back side with a needle-turn stitch as is done today. Corners may be mitered or butted.

To assemble a Potholder quilt of several blocks, join two blocks together with whipstitching from the back very near the edge of the finished blocks. Although this stitching will generally show on the back, on the front the bindings should look like sashing with a quilting line running down the center.

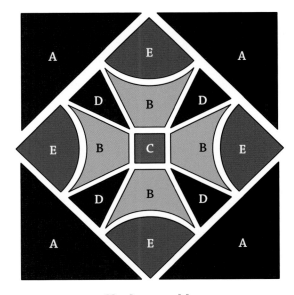

Block assembly

Greek Cross
Don Beld

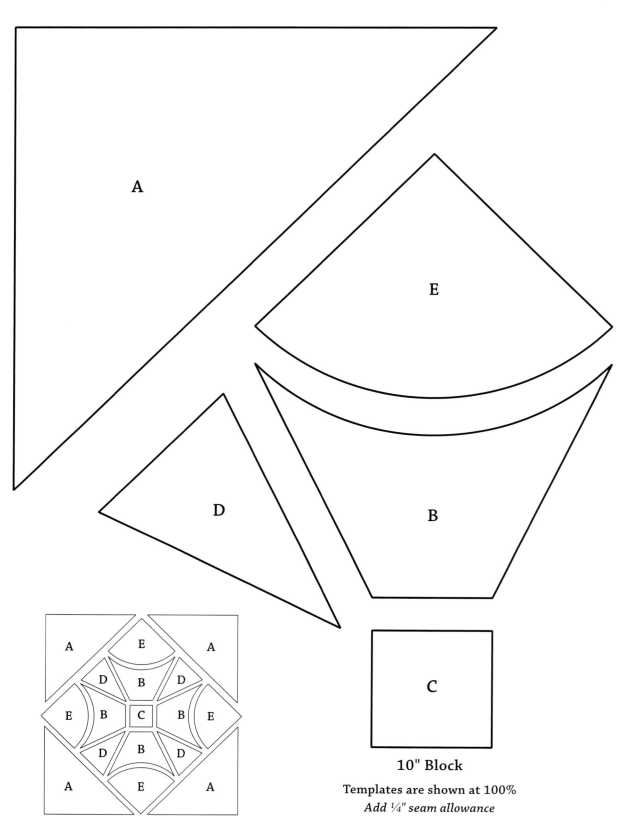

10" Block

Templates are shown at 100%

Add ¼" seam allowance

men and the art of QUILTMAKING ▸◂ JOE CUNNINGHAM

Richard **Caro**

KING'S RANSOM, 72" x 72", **2009**. Made by Richard Caro.

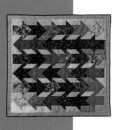

KING'S RANSOM
Richard Caro

This quilt design arose out of a fat quarter swap on the online QuiltGuy Yahoo group. We ended up with 14 purple and 14 gold fat quarters. This design seemed like a great way to use the fabric and also realize an idea I'd been carrying around in my mind for years.

I brought the fat quarters with me to a Quilt-Guy retreat in August 2008 and cut and assembled the fabric over the weekend. It was fun to get everyone's input and feedback on the various color layouts and arrangements. I chose to go with some color symmetry and also some random color selections. The negative and positive effect is increased if the two color groups have enough light and value contrast.

The quilt I made is approximately 72" x 72". Your quilt can be larger or smaller depending on how many pattern repeats are used. The instructions here have been simplified, so your quilt will look more like the schematic (Fig. 1) than the quilt photo, but you can always do what I did and improvise until you get what you like.

The quilt is a pretty good fat quarter quilt. I chose to use 14 fat quarters for the purple arrows and 14 for the background gold fabric. This provides enough fabric for two complete arrows from each fat quarter and more than enough for the background. That said, you can use fewer background fat quarters and repeat the fabrics in more places. Border, binding, and backing are the quiltmaker's choice.

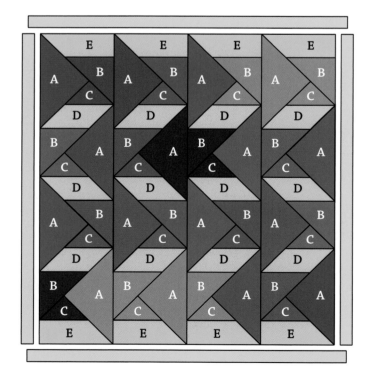

Fig. 1

The pattern, in regards to the colors of the arrows, needs to be laid out beforehand so that the tails of the arrows in one column of blocks matches up with the points of the arrows in the next column. It is helpful to lay out the entire design and manipulate color choices and then sew so that the tails of the arrows and the points of the arrows don't get confused. Look at the quilt photo for guidance.

For the triangular blocks sew templates B, C, and D together to make a unit to be sewn to template A. Eight of these blocks will "point" left, eight will point right. Reverse D as needed to go in the correct direction (Figs. 2–4).

Join a template E and B piece and attach to two triangle units to make the top left and top right corners (Fig. 5). Join a C and E piece and attach to two triangle units to make the bottom left and bottom right corners (Fig. 6).

Join four triangles per column and make four columns, noting the placement of the corner units. Join the columns and trim away excess fabric to even the bottom edge. You can add a border or two at this point if you like.

I chose to hand quilt two rows of stitches around the insides of the arrows. The first row I stitched along the seam allowance, approximately ¼" from the seam and the next row ¼" inside of the first line, or approximately ½" away from the seam. I stuck to the edge of the arrow as defined by the color and not by the pieces of fabric that make up the arrow, so, I stitched across some seams. I chose to use one row of stitches in the background blocks.

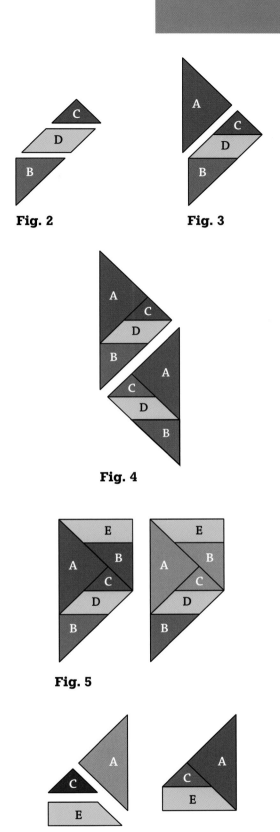

Fig. 2

Fig. 3

Fig. 4

Fig. 5

Fig. 6

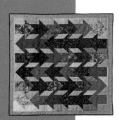

KING'S RANSOM
Richard Caro

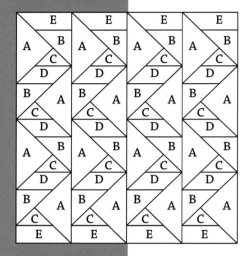

Templates are shown at 100%
Add ¼" seam allowance

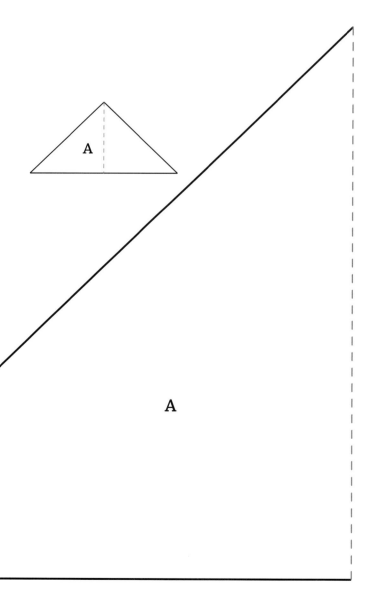

KING'S RANSOM
Richard Caro

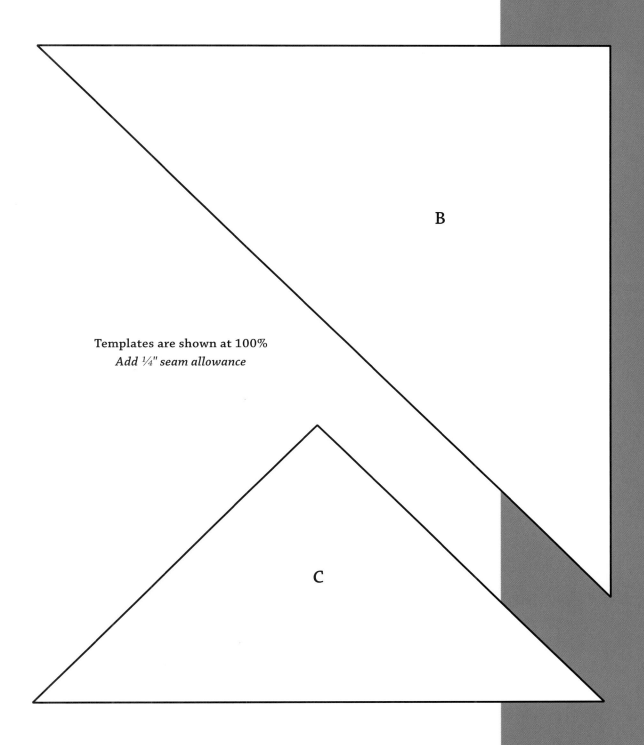

B

Templates are shown at 100%
Add ¼" seam allowance

C

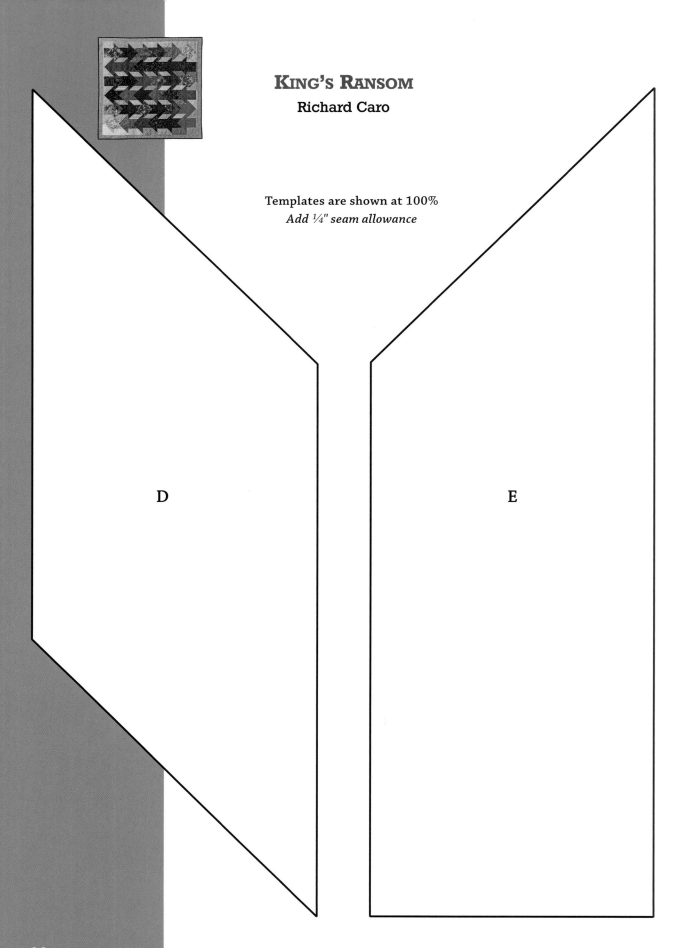

KING'S RANSOM
Richard Caro

Templates are shown at 100%
Add ¼" seam allowance

D

E

Joe **Cunningham**

SNAKE IN THE GARDEN, 66" x 66", 2000.
Made by Joe Cunningham.

SNAKE IN THE GARDEN
Joe Cunningham

Fig. 1

men and the art of QUILTMAKING ▸•◂ JOE CUNNINGHAM

SNAKE IN THE GARDEN
Joe Cunningham

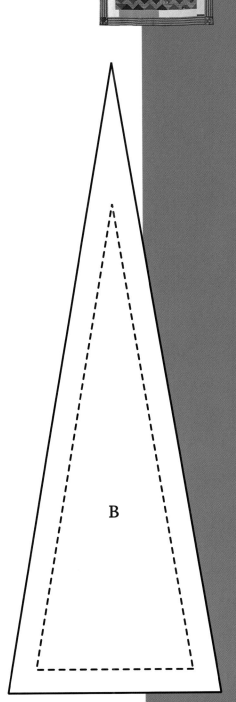

I built SNAKE IN THE GARDEN from section A outward, usually making extra lengths of each border so I could simply cut off what I did not need.

For the central spiral (A) I cut two 27½" squares, one yellow, and one blue and white. I laid the yellow square right-side up on top of the right side of the blue-and-white square. Starting in the very middle, I basted the two squares together in a spiral from the center out, trying to keep the basting lines about 1½" apart as I went. When I reached the edge of the fabric, I used scissors to cut the yellow fabric round and round between the basting lines all the way back to the middle. Then, using a straw needle and matching thread, I turned the edge under as I worked to hand appliqué the edge from the middle clear out to the end of the tail, around its tip and back down to the middle. Because the fabric was cut round and round, sometimes the cut was on the bias and sometimes it was on the straight grain. Also, I had created the entire spiral freehand, with no markings. Those two factors combined to make my "snake" irregular and asymmetrical. You can see how its "body" grows thicker and thinner in places; how it sometimes has angles where there should be curves.

Another way to create the center spiral would be to work with a length of bias. To keep the snake about ¾" wide, cut the bias from the fabric of your choice about 1½" wide. You will need approximately 15 yards. Baste the spiral in place from the center outward. Add a circle to the middle to indicate the head and allow the tail end to taper toward the tip.

For the first border (B) I used this full-sized template B with seam allowances as shown and cut 68 dark triangles and 68 light triangles. I pressed carefully the same way each time as I sewed them into strips of 18 light and 18 dark. I pressed the finished strips, then cut them to 27½" lengths, ignoring where the triangles started and stopped at the ends.

B

Template B shown at 100%

SNAKE IN THE GARDEN
Joe Cunningham

Fig. 2

From the scraps I created four corner squares with random crazy patches, large enough that I could trim them down to 5¾" squares (5¼" finished.) To add the borders, I started with the sides, adding only the pieced borders, no corner squares. Then I added the 5¼" crazy corners to the remaining two pieced sections, pinned the junctions to align the corner squares, then pinned the rest carefully and sewed it all in place to complete border B (Fig. 2).

Border C is made of only one triangle, 7¼" on its long side. Since I wanted the long sides to be on the straight of the grain, I cut the triangles in groups of four by starting out with an 8½" square, then cutting it diagonally both ways. That way the short edges were all on the bias. (Making the square 8½" allows for the seam allowances all around, so the finished triangles can be 7¼".) To create the zigzag effect, I made every other triangle from a light blue stripe. First I sewed lengths of alternating colors, one blue and one brown, red, or green (Fig. 3). Since I was going to add the side borders first, I made extra length and simply cut it square at 38½".

Fig. 3

Create the zigzag borders first. Cut the ends square at 38½" or to match your dimensions of finished border B (Fig. 4).

Add the top and bottom sections.

Border D is a simple scrap border 4¾" wide (finished). Mine is made mostly of unbleached muslin, with scraps thrown in for variety. On this border I added the top and bottom sections first. Before I sewed them on, I made sure they were the same length, so my quilt remained square (Fig. 5).

For border E I followed my usual procedure of cutting all four borders the same length to maintain my dimensions. They are 5½" finished. The long pieces of striped material are 61½" by 5½" finished. The corner squares are 5½" square. If your quilt is slightly larger or smaller at this point, just make all four sides the same to match your quilt.

For the binding I cut bias from my scraps 1⅜" wide, in various lengths. I machine stitched it to the face of the quilt, turned it over to the back and whipstitched it down.

Fig. 4

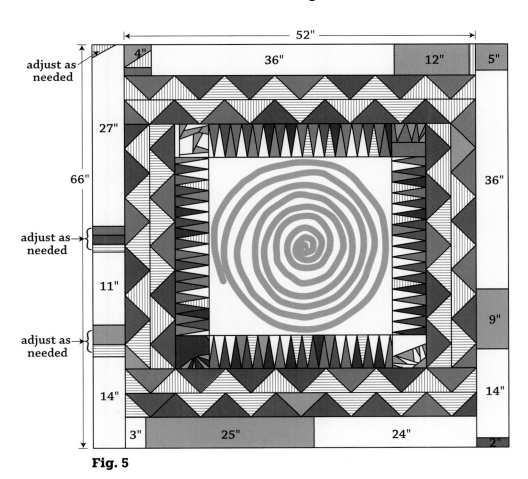

Fig. 5

Joe Cunningham
(Standing in for Ernest B. Haight)

FALLING BLOCKS, 74½" x 90½", 1964.
Made by Ernest B. Haight (1899-1986).

FALLING BLOCKS

Ernest B. Haight

(re-drafted and explained by Joe Cunningham)

Ernest created this original pattern for a quilt given to the Reverend and Mrs. Albert J. Larsen in 1964 by members of the First Baptist Church of David City, Nebraska. The many embroidered signatures on the quilt surely belong to church members, but the bottom border is all Ernest.

The actual quilt has measurements other quilters are not likely to recreate successfully, so my suggestion is to come as close as you can, trim the blocks to fit as best as possible, and let the obvious playfulness and whimsy of the original allow you to let go of perfect points and complete accuracy.

 First, cut random strips and piece them together to make blocks A (6½" x 7½") and B (5½" x 6½"). To make a quilt as large as Ernest's, you will need 30 of each.

 Next, cut 30 squares each of blocks C (6½" x 7½") and D (5½" x 6½"). Ernest used a mix of solids and prints for these blocks.

 Assemble A – D as shown in the diagram (Fig. 1) and trim to 12" square. Then add 4 E triangles or 4 Er triangles to each block so you have an even number of blocks that "tip" left and right.

 Following the photo, sew the blocks together, five to a row, alternating the way each block tips. Sew the six rows together. Add a border (Ernest's was 2¾" wide when finished). Quilt as desired (Ernest used a 1½" x 1½" diamond grid allover pattern) and bind.

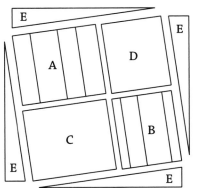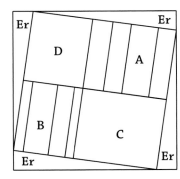

Fig. 1

FALLING BLOCKS

Ernest B. Haight

(re-drafted and explained by Joe Cunningham)

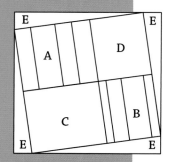

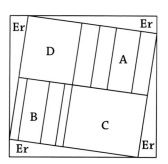

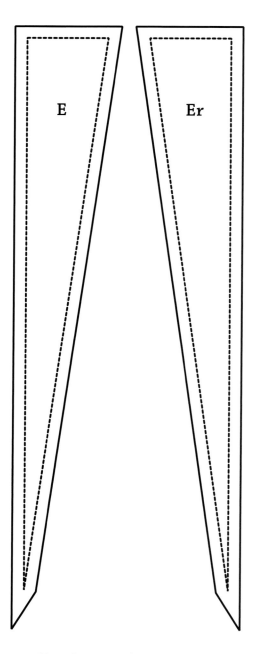

Templates are shown at 50%

Enlarge 200%

Joe **Cunningham**

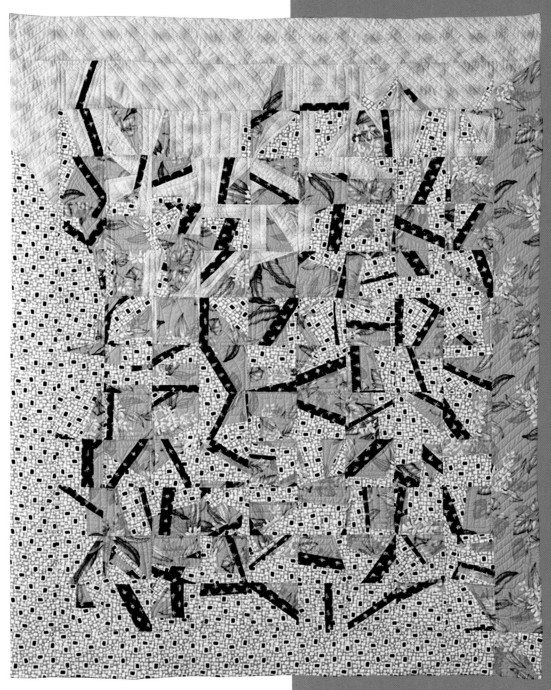

CUBIST ROSE, 58½" x 76½", 2009.
Made by Joe Cunningham.

CUBIST ROSE

Joe Cunningham

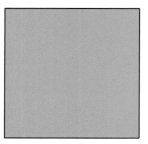

Step 1

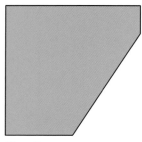

Step 2

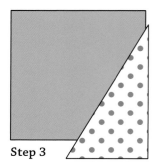

Step 3

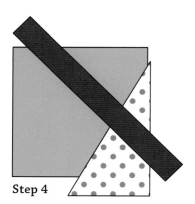

Step 4

Step 5

Here is the way I created this quilt:

First I picked four fabrics: pink for the flowers, green for the foliage, blue for the sky, and black for the sticks and stems.

Second, I followed a set of steps to create blocks:

- Cut a 6" x 6" square of pink.
- Cut off one corner.
- Replace the corner with another fabric.
- Cut the resulting rough square somewhere and insert a black strip.
- Using a 6" square ruler, trim the block to 6" with a rotary cutter.

Keep starting with one of the three colors and repeat the process in a different way each time. As you work you will see that you need three distinct groups of blocks:

those with more pink,

those with more green, and

those with more blue.

Any block you make will work into your design. After you have 50 or 60 blocks you can lay them out and see how you need to arrange them to suggest a landscape—if you like—or simply an abstract design you find pleasing.

I allowed the process to change radically as I worked. That is, sometimes I had no black strip; sometimes I used only two fabrics in a block, etc.

Finally, I added 6" borders of my three colors. I machine quilted straight lines in the borders and maze-like designs in the center blocks. When I was done the finished quilt was 58½" x 76½".

Scott Hansen

BASKET CASE NO. 1, 48½" x 50½", 2009.
Designed, pieced, and quilted by Scott Hansen.

BASKET CASE No. 1
Scott Hansen

I would love to see how you interpret this quilt... Drop me a line at **bluenickel5@earthlink.net** so you can share your version with me or to ask any questions you may have. Keep Sewing, Keep Happy!

Fabric

Assorted Red Prints totaling 1 yard
Assorted Black Prints totaling 1 yard
Assorted Cream Prints totaling 1 yard
1 yard Cream Print for setting squares
½ yard Black Print for cornerstones
1 yard Red Print for sashing strips
1 yard Red Print for binding
3 yards backing fabric of your choice (or less
    if you include your scraps from the front;
    there will likely be leftover fabric)
54" x 54" batting

In all instructions ¼" seams are assumed throughout this pattern.

Cutting the Pieces

FOR THE BASKET BLOCKS

Cut (90) 2⅞" squares (Piece A) of assorted Cream Prints. Cut in half once diagonally for 180 half-square triangles.

Cut (45) 2⅞" squares (Piece A) of assorted Black Prints. Cut in half once diagonally for 90 half-square triangles.

Cut (45) 2⅞" squares (Piece A) of assorted Red Prints. Cut in half once diagonally for 90 half-square triangles.

Cut (72) 2½" x 4½" rectangles (Piece B) of assorted Cream Prints.

FOR THE SETTING SQUARE BLOCKS

Cut (25) 4½" squares (Piece C) of Cream Print for setting squares.

Cut (100) 1½" squares (Piece D) of Black Print for cornerstones.

Cut (100) 1½" x 4½" pieces (Piece E) of Red Print for sashing strips.

FOR THE SIDE SETTING TRIANGLE BLOCKS

Cut (5) 7" squares (Piece F) cut in half twice diagonally for 20 quarter-square triangles.

Cut (60) 1½" squares (Piece D) of Black Print for cornerstones.

Cut (40) 1½" x 4½" pieces (Piece E) of Red Print for sashing strips.

FOR THE CORNER SETTING TRIANGLE BLOCKS

Cut (2) 3¾" squares (Piece G) cut in half once diagonally for 4 half-square triangles.

Cut (8) 1½" squares (Piece D) of Black Print for cornerstones.

Cut (4) 1½" x 4½" pieces (Piece E) of Red Print for sashing strips.

Sewing the Blocks Together

Before you begin piecing the blocks, understand that a random look, as in the quilt I made, is not necessarily easy or may not be what you want. You can follow the fabric placement exactly as I have in the photo, or you may choose your own. At any rate have fun with it, and expect that no matter how hard you try to make it random...sometimes prints just end up next to each other or cause a little sub-pattern on their own.

Sewing the Basket Blocks Together

 Sew all of the Cream (Piece A) half-square triangles to the Red and Black (Piece A) half-square triangles, creating 90 units of Red/Cream and 90 units of Black/Cream.

Separate into piles of 60 all Red/Cream, 60 all Black/Cream, and 60 of both Red/Cream and Black/Cream units.

From each pile create 12 Basket blocks as follows, referring to the photo of the quilt and the diagrams:

Sew 2 units together.

Then repeat with 2 more units.

Sew these 2 new units together.

Then sew 1 Cream piece B to the side.

Now sew 1 Cream piece B to the side of 1 unit.

Sew these 2 units together.

Sewing the Setting Squares Together

Sew 2 Black piece Ds to each end of a Red piece E.

Repeat with 2 more piece Ds and 1 piece E.

Sew 2 Red piece Es to both sides of 1 Cream piece C.

Sew these 3 units together.

Sewing the Side Setting Triangles Together

Sew 1 Black piece D to 1 Red piece E.

Sew this unit to one of the short sides of a Cream piece F.

Sew 2 Black piece Ds to each end of 1 Red Print piece E.

BASKET CASE NO. 1
Scott Hansen

▣ Sew this unit to the other side of the Cream piece F.

SEWING THE CORNER SETTING TRIANGLES TOGETHER

▣ Sew 2 Black piece Ds to each end of 1 Red Print piece E.

▣ Sew this unit to the long side of a Cream piece G.

Putting It All Together

▣ Sew the Basket Blocks, Setting Blocks, and Side Setting Triangles in rows.

▣ When done piecing the top together, trim off the Black cornerstones around the edge of the whole top, being sure to leave a ¼" seam allowance for attaching the binding.

▣ Quilt the top and bind it with your favorite method using the 1 yard of Red Print.

▣ Don't forget to include a label!! And if you would like to add a picture of your project to the Blue Nickel Studios flickr page, I would be most delighted: **www.flickr.com/groups/1294513@N23**. ▣

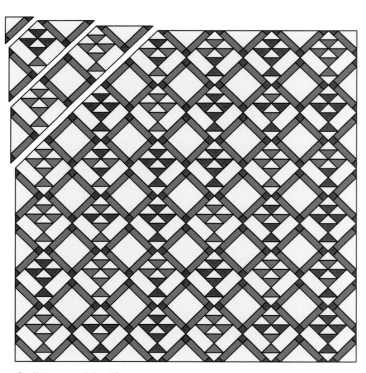

Quilt assembly diagram

Raymond K. **Houston**

LOLLOO/P4/II, 90" x 60", ©2006. Made by
Raymond K. Houston.

Lolloo/P4/II

Raymond K. Houston

This rather spiky windmill is a tessellation, a single shape that fits with itself to cover the surface of the quilt. It is actually easier than it looks. The pattern is generated from one 15" block, colored six different ways.

The Templates

Make templates A through E (pages 100–101).

The Fabrics

2¼ yards of Orange fabric
4⅜ yards of Blue fabric
6½ yards of White fabric

The Cutting

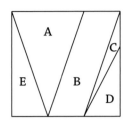

From the Orange fabric, cut 16 each of pieces A, B, C, D, and E.

From the Blue fabric, cut 32 each of pieces A, B, C, D, and E.

From the White fabric, cut 48 each of pieces A, B, C, D, and E.

The Blocks

(Use a ¼" seam allowance and sew right sides together.)

Sew piece B to piece A pressing the seam allowance toward piece B.

Sew piece C to piece B pressing the seam allowance toward piece C.

Sew piece D to piece C pressing the seam allowance toward piece D.

Sew piece E to piece A pressing the seam allowance toward piece E.

Orange/White Blocks A (O/W A). Sew 4 blocks colored as shown and sew them together. Make 4 of these 4-Patch blocks.

 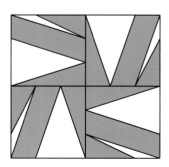

Orange/White Blocks B (O/W B). Sew 4 blocks colored as shown and sew them together. Make 2 of these 4-Patch blocks.

 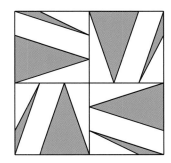

Blue/White Blocks B (B/W B). Sew 4 blocks colored as shown and sew them together. Make 6 of these 4-Patch blocks.

 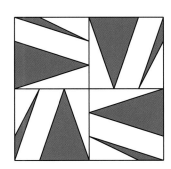

Orange/White/Blue Transition Blocks (O/W/B T). Sew 4 blocks colored as shown and sew them together. Take note of the exact color placement. Make 4 of these 4-Patch blocks.

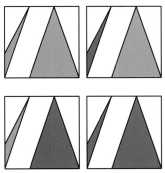 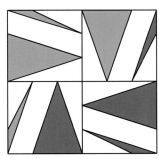

The Arrangement

Arrange the blocks as shown. The Orange/White and Blue/White Blocks look the same no matter how you rotate them, but the Orange/White/Blue Transition Blocks must be arranged with the Orange/White patch in the upper left corner and the Blue/White patch in the lower right corner. ◧

Blue/White Blocks A (B/W A). Sew 4 blocks colored as shown and sew them together. Make 8 of these 4-Patch blocks.

 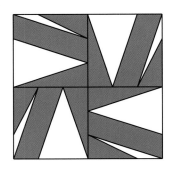

O/W A	O/W B	O/W A	O/W B T	B/W A	B/W B
O/W B	O/W A	O/W B T	B/W A	B/W B	B/W A
O/W A	O/W B T	B/W A	B/W B	B/W A	B/W B
O/W B T	B/W A	B/W B	B/W A	B/W B	B/W A

Block assembly diagram

Lolloo/P4/II

Raymond K. Houston

Templates are shown at 100%

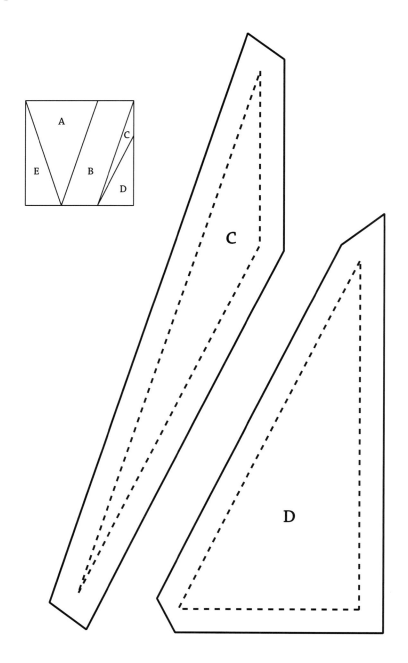

men and the art of QUILTMAKING ►•◄ JOE CUNNINGHAM

LOLLOO/P4/II
Raymond K. Houston

Templates are shown at 100%

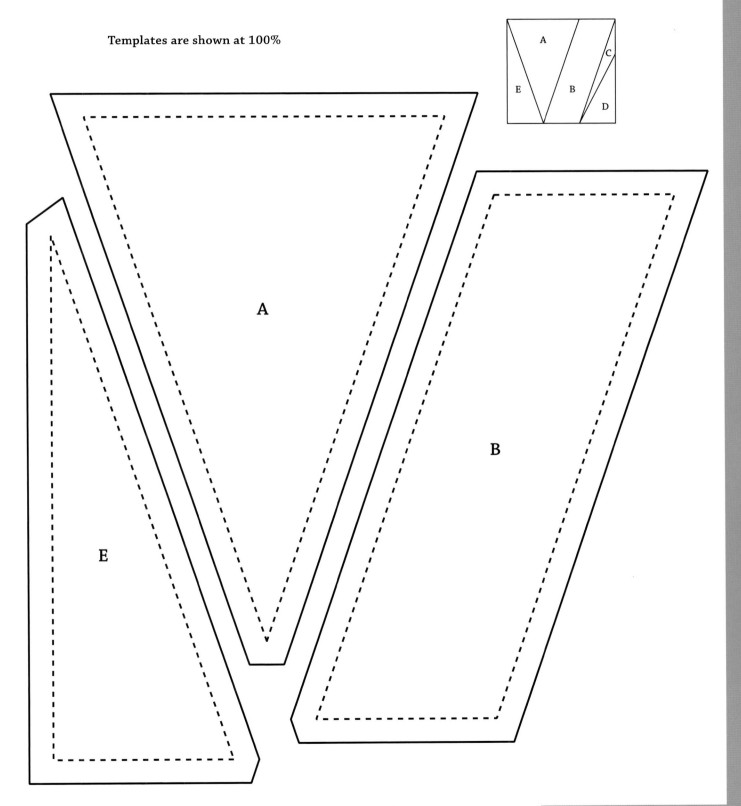

Michael **Kashey**

WHAT'S IN A NAME: ROSE WINDOW TREE

Michael Kashey

Calligraphy is seldom used in quilting. In fact, using penmanship as aesthetic design is unusual in Western art. But I've been intrigued since childhood with calligraphy's flowing strokes, angles, and curves. So, with German Scherenschnitte, Polish Wycinanki, and Oriental paper cutwork as inspiration, I created this quilt, combining family signatures in an unusual way. This is the process to create my version of a Rose Window block:

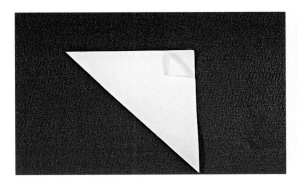

A square of thin paper is folded in half diagonally to form a right-angle triangle.

Shown here are a blank 30-degree wedge cut from paper and a completed wedge with the written name "Mike."

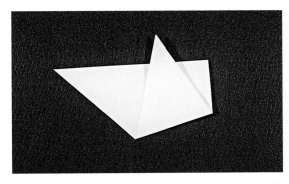

Divide the hypotenuse long side of the triangle into three 60-degree sections and fold one section as shown. Turn over.

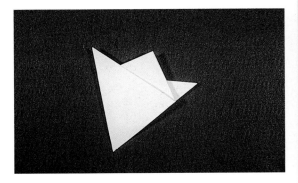

Turn the other 60-degree section to form a 60-degree triangle.

OPPOSITE: **WHAT'S IN A NAME: ROSE WINDOW TREE, 61" x 95", 2004. Made by Michael Kashey.**

WHAT'S IN A NAME: ROSE WINDOW TREE

Michael Kashey

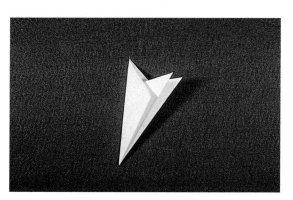

Fold the triangle in half, forming a 30-60-90 degree triangle as shown. Write the name across this wedge, making sure some letters touch top and bottom folds. Cut out the design as you would a snowflake.

The drawn, cut, and unfolded radial pattern repeats "Mike" and its mirror image six times.

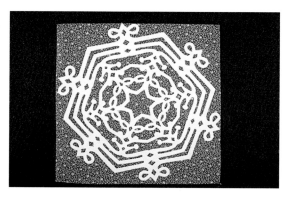

A freezer-paper pattern made from the design is ironed onto patterned appliqué fabric.

The light background fabric is revealed after the appliqué is complete.

Dye, paint, embroider—do what you will with the appliquéd blocks. ▪

The quilt project appeared in more detail in American Quilter: Projects 2005, *which is available online to AQS members at:* www.americanquilter.com. *Choose* American Quilter *magazine; choose show all articles; choose member-only articles; choose p.31.*

Scott Murkin

AUTUMN COMES TO DELECTABLE MOUNTAINS,
84" x 84", 2003. Made by Scott Murkin.

AUTUMN COMES TO
DELECTABLE MOUNTAINS
Scott Murkin

Fabric amounts only cover the top; add additional fabric for backing. Add 90" x 90" batting.

Burgundy Print: 3 yards (add ¾ yard if binding with the same fabric)

CUT:

NOTE: All subsequent cuts to make half-square (once) or quarter-square triangles (twice) are on the diagonal.

A – 1 @ 3½" x 3½"
B – 56 @ 3⅞" x 3⅞" (cut once = 112)
C – 56 @ 2⅞" x 2⅞" (cut once = 112)
D – 4 @ 1½" x 1½"
E – 67 @ 3¼" x 3¼" (cut twice = 268)
F – 8 @ 1⅞" x 1⅞" (cut once = 16)
G – 2 @ 9¼" x 9¼" (cut twice = 8)
H – 2 @ 6⅞" x 6⅞" (cut once = 4)
J – 2 @ 21¼" x 21¼" (cut twice = 8)
K – 2 @ 18⅞" x 18⅞" (cut once = 4)

(There are no letters I or Q.)

Cream Print: 5 yards

CUT:

L – 1 @ 4¼" x 4¼" (cut twice = 4)
E – 68 @ 3¼" x 3¼" (cut twice = 272)
F – 12 @ 1⅞" x 1⅞" (cut once = 24)
M – 4 @ 4½" x 4½"
G – 1 @ 9¼" x 9¼" (cut twice = 4)
N – 4 @ 1½" x 18½"
O – 1 @ 11¼" x 11¼" (cut twice = 4)
C – 60 @ 2⅞" x 2⅞" (cut once = 120)
P – 4 @ 6½" x 42½"
R – 1 @ 23¼" x 23¼" (cut twice = 4)
S – 4 @ 6½" x 78½"
B – 54 @ 3⅞" x 3⅞" (cut once = 108)

Use the two diagrams for assembly directions. Avoid inset seams by sewing partial seams where necessary.

This quilt looks best when all three Cream borders are mitered, to preserve design symmetry. ▰

AUTUMN COMES TO
DELECTABLE MOUNTAINS
Scott Murkin

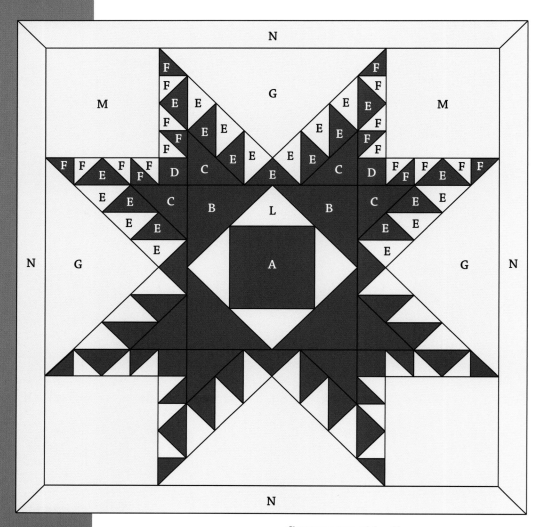

Center assembly diagram

QUILT INDEX

QUILTMAKERS INDEX

The Men

THE AUTHOR

Joe Cunningham grew up in Flint, Michigan. He started playing guitar and drums at an early age and began playing music professionally in high school. He made his living from music until he was invited to write the catalogue for a quilt documentation project.

To prepare for that he learned how to make quilts, and since 1979 he has been making, writing about, talking and teaching about, and even singing about quilts. From the beginning, Joe has been a student of quilt history, writing scholarly articles, essays, and books on the subject.

In his studies he ran across the story of Joe the Quilter, an Englishman who made quilts in the late 1700s. This story inspired him to create a one-man musical quilt show called "Joe the Quilter" comprised of songs, stories, and original quilts all created to tell the tale of the original Joe. In 2001 Joe added the show to his repertoire of lectures and classes, leading to performances throughout the country.

Today Joe lives in San Francisco with his wife and sons, working from his quilt studio in the city, and living in the Presidio National Park, the former Army base adjacent to the Golden Gate Bridge.

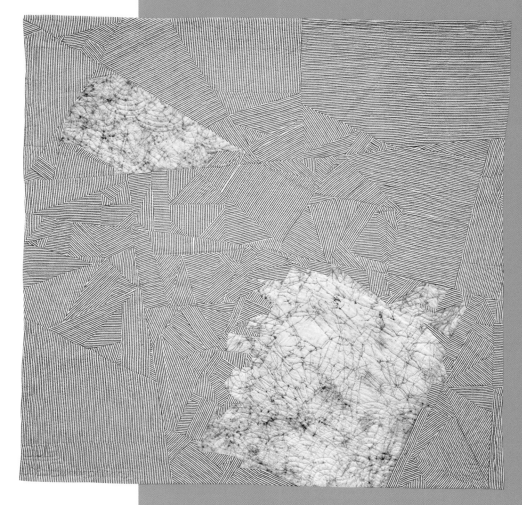

ISLAND IN TWO PARTS, 72" x 72", 2010. Made by the author.

other AQS books

For today's quilter...
inspiration and creativity from

AQS Publishing